A LETTER FROM PETER MUNK

Since we started the Munk Debates, my wife, Melanie, and I have been deeply gratified at how quickly they have captured the public's imagination. From the time of our first event in May 2008, we have hosted what I believe are some of the most exciting public policy debates in Canada and internationally. Global in focus, the Munk Debates have tackled a range of issues, such as humanitarian intervention, the effectiveness of foreign aid, the threat of global warming, religion's impact on geopolitics, the rise of China, and the decline of Europe. These compelling topics have served as intellectual and ethical grist for some of the world's most important thinkers and doers, from Henry Kissinger to Tony Blair, Christopher Hitchens to Paul Krugman, Lord Peter Mandelson to Fareed Zakaria.

The issues raised at the Munk Debates have not only fostered public awareness, but they have also helped many of us become more involved and, therefore, less intimidated by the concept of globalization. It is so easy to be inward-looking. It is so easy to be xenophobic. It is so easy to be nationalistic. It is hard to go into the unknown. Globalization, for many people, is an abstract concept at best. The purpose of this debate series is to help people feel more familiar with our fast-changing world and more comfortable participating in the universal dialogue about the issues and events that will shape our collective future.

I don't need to tell you that that there are many, many burning issues. Global warming, the blight of extreme poverty, genocide, or our shaky financial order: these are just a few of the critical issues that matter to people. And it seems to me, and to my foundation board members, that the quality of the public dialogue on these critical issues diminishes in direct proportion to the salience and number of these issues clamouring for our attention. By trying to highlight the most important issues at crucial moments in the global conversation, these debates not only profile the ideas and opinions of some of the world's brightest thinkers, but they also crystallize public passion and knowledge, helping to tackle some of the challenges confronting humankind.

I have learned in life — and I'm sure many of you will share this view — that challenges bring out the best in us. I hope you'll agree that the participants in these debates challenge not only each other but also each of us to think clearly and logically about important problems facing our world.

Peter Munk
Founder, Aurea Foundation
Toronto, Ontario

HAS OBAMA MADE THE WORLD A MORE DANGEROUS PLACE?

STEPHENS AND KAGAN VS. ZAKARIA AND SLAUGHTER

THE MUNK DEBATE ON U.S. FOREIGN POLICY

Edited by Rudyard Griffiths

ANANSI

This edition published in 2015 by
House of Anansi Press Inc.
110 Spadina Avenue, Suite 801
Toronto, ON, M5V 2K4
Tel. 416-363-4343
Fax 416-363-1017
www.houseofanansi.com

Distributed in Canada by
HarperCollins Canada Ltd.
1995 Markham Road
Scarborough, ON, M1B 5M8
Toll free tel. 1-800-387-0117

Distributed in the United States by
Publishers Group West
1700 Fourth Street
Berkeley, CA, 94710
Toll free tel. 1-800-788-3123

House of Anansi Press is committed to protecting our natural environment.
As part of our efforts, the interior of this book is printed on paper that contains 100%
post-consumer recycled fibres, is acid-free, and is processed chlorine-free.

19 18 17 16 15   1 2 3 4 5

Library and Archives Canada Cataloguing in Publication
Has Obama made the world a more dangerous place?: Stephens and Kagan vs. Zakaria and
Slaughter: the Munk debate on U.S. foreign policy / edited by Rudyard Griffiths.

(The Munk debates)
Issued in print and electronic formats.
ISBN: 978-1-77089-996-4 (pbk.). ISBN: 978-1-77089-997-1 (html).

1. United States — Foreign relations — 2009–. I. Stephens, Bret, 1973—,
panelist II. Kagan, Robert, panelist III. Zakaria, Fareed, panelist
IV. Slaughter, Anne-Marie, panelist V. Griffiths, Rudyard, editor
VI. Series: Munk debates

E907.H38 2015   973.932   C2014-906996-0
                                           C2014-906997-9

Library of Congress Control Number: 2014953296

Cover design: Alysia Shewchuk
Typesetting: Laura Brady

Canada Council   Conseil des Arts   ONTARIO ARTS COUNCIL
for the Arts   du Canada   CONSEIL DES ARTS DE L'ONTARIO

*We acknowledge for their financial support of our publishing program
the Canada Council for the Arts, the Ontario Arts Council, and the Government of Canada
through the Canada Book Fund.*

Printed and bound in Canada

MIX
Paper from
responsible sources
FSC® C004071
www.fsc.org

CONTENTS

INTRODUCTION BY RUDYARD GRIFFITHS

Has the foreign policy of President Barack Obama made the world a more dangerous place? This simple question animated a fiercely contested debate in the autumn of 2014 that featured some of the world's top thinkers on the state and future of U.S. foreign policy. It also riveted a public audience of 3,000 people in Toronto, Canada, and thousands more watching online. For the debaters and audiences alike the issue at hand was how much President Obama and his administration were responsible for a wave of geopolitical instability that had reverberated from the Middle East to Eastern Europe to China and the Asia-Pacific region in the preceding months. Were the violent actions of ISIL (Islamic State of Iraq and Syria and the Levant), Vladimir Putin, Bashar al-Assad, and those of a host of other bad actors being stoked by a president whose failed foreign policy has carelessly emboldened the West's enemies? Or was no one nation, let alone a solitary U.S. president, the cause of the kinds of geopolitical instability and great power rivalries that increasingly define our multi-polar world? Do presidents make history, forming through the adroit use of American power oases of stability and prosperity out of the chaos of global events? Or is every U.S. administration the product of global trends and the international balance of power, allowing presidents to at best nudge the course of history and world events in a better direction?

Arguing for a critical assessment of the effectiveness of Barack Obama's execution of U.S. foreign policy were Bret Stephens and Robert Kagan. Bret Stephens honed his razor-sharp attacks on the Obama presidency's impact on world events as the deputy editorial page editor for the international opinion pages of the *Wall Street Journal* and as author of the paper's weekly foreign affairs column, "Global View." Robert Kagan was the debate's consummate foreign policy insider. In addition to being a senior fellow at the prestigious Brookings Institution, he has been an influential and bipartisan adviser to the top echelons of U.S. leadership, including Hillary Clinton, John McCain, and George W. Bush.

Throughout the debate Bret pushed home the point that President Obama was the author of his and the world's misfortunes by not having the United States assume its traditional role as the dominant global power: "There were no consequences for Assad in Syria, no real consequences for Putin in Georgia or Ukraine; and the rogues of the world sensed that we now live in a place where no one is in charge, where the United States is afraid to intervene in all circumstances, which allows them to do whatever they want. We're entering into a broken-windows world. We need a foreign policy that understands that the role of a great power is to maintain order as a policeman, not as a priest."

Robert Kagan took a different tack in his criticism of the president. His concern was not simply with the crises of the moment but with the continued erosion of the liberal democratic international order under President Obama: "I am worried that if we're not careful, we will, through lack of action, through misunderstanding, and through foolishness, lose control of a liberal order from which we've all benefited so much. And let me tell you, it is fragile. [Zakaria] thinks this liberal world order will go on forever . . . And do you know why, according to Fareed? Because China will step up and uphold it. Because Russia will step up. Or India and Brazil. The rise of the rest! They'll come in and uphold the liberal world order even after the United States has lost the power." For Bret Stephens and Robert Kagan, the president's foreign policy was a failure not only in the particular instances of Ukraine, Syria, and Iraq but also in the broader context of defending the liberal values and norms that underwrote the postwar order.

Defending President Obama's foreign policy at the debate were two forceful advocates for a nuanced analysis of global affairs, one that acknowledges how international relations itself have changed in new and complex ways.

Anne-Marie Slaughter served at the highest levels of

the U.S. State Department under Hillary Clinton and has had a distinguished career as a scholar of international relations. As the head of New America, one of America's top international affairs think tanks, she is a sought-after commentator on world events. Her debating partner was CNN television host Fareed Zakaria. An acclaimed author, broadcaster, and active participant in foreign policy conversations, he is one of the most effective and versatile debaters of his generation.

During the debate Anne-Marie Slaughter skilfully pressured Robert Kagan and Bret Stephens to prove how President Obama, as a single person, was responsible for global flashpoints as diverse as the situations in Syria and Eastern Ukraine, tensions between China and Japan, and the lacklustre global response to climate change. In Slaughter's assessment: "Blaming Barack Obama for the state that the world is in right now is like blaming a Caribbean island for a hurricane. Think very carefully about what our opponents have to prove. Not only do they have to prove that the world would be less dangerous if Barack Obama were not president, but they have to prove that the world is as dangerous as it is because he has emboldened our enemies." Some of the debate's best clashes revolved around this thesis and the critiques offered up by Bret Stephens and Robert Kagan for why Obama should not be let off so easily.

Fareed Zakaria's contribution to the debate focused on praising the president's cautious use of American power as a hallmark of how a more mature and realistic U.S. foreign policy had evolved under Obama's leadership:

"[Kagan's] problem with the Syrian intervention is that it is not vigorous enough. He wants Obama to do it more wholeheartedly, with lots of troops, and maybe ground forces, like we did in Iraq, which worked out so well. Yes, I was one of the people who originally thought that getting rid of Saddam Hussein was a good idea. But with $2 trillion, 175,000 troops, 5,000 troops dead, and 400,000 Iraqis perhaps dead and wounded later, I learned something, and I don't want to replicate that lesson in Syria, the neighbouring country." Together, Anne-Marie and Fareed pushed their opponents to make the case that another president, faced with similar circumstances, would have been able to respond to the complex crises that faced the Obama administration in ways that lessened conflict and increased stability — no easy feat by anyone's measure.

In addition to the specific arguments in favour of or against the idea of the Obama presidency making the world a more dangerous place, this debate provides important insights into the contested terrain that is America's role in the world. Do we still live in an era where a single power, equipped with overwhelming economic and military might, can and should shape global events? More fundamentally, is such an assertive role on the world stage not simply an option that presidents can adopt or discard but a core responsibility for America in the twenty-first century? Bret Stephens and Robert Kagan would answer these questions with a resounding "yes." For them, this has been and always will be America's global role.

Yet a significant number of nations and people, including many Americans, think that such a heavy burden is neither realistic nor desirable for a single country or president. Instead, like Fareed Zakaria and Anne-Marie Slaughter, they would argue that the world is becoming ever more interconnected and interdependent. America's role should be to foster international co-operation, regional dialogue, and strong global institutions that allow this process to deepen and strengthen with U.S. assistance, but not because America has imposed an international order through superior military and economic might.

Which one of these visions for America's role in world affairs will win out? At this moment of flux in the international balance of power it is anyone's guess. This debate will provide readers with a wide-ranging understanding of the high stakes involved in this global conversation for both America and the world. We know that where the United States and the international community ultimately come down on this issue will define much of how we live and experience world events in the coming decades.

Rudyard Griffiths
Organizer and Moderator, the Munk Debates
Toronto, Ontario

Has Obama Made the World a More Dangerous Place?

Pro: Bret Stephens and Robert Kagan
Con: Fareed Zakaria and Anne-Marie Slaughter

November 5, 2014
Toronto, Ontario

THE MUNK DEBATE ON U.S. FOREIGN POLICY

RUDYARD GRIFFITHS: Good evening, everyone. Welcome to the Munk Debate on Barack Obama's foreign policy. I'm Rudyard Griffiths and it's my privilege to be the organizer of this debate series and to once again serve as your moderator. I want to start tonight by welcoming the North America–wide radio and television audience tuning into this debate from the Canadian Broadcasting Corporation (CBC), to CPAC, Canada's public affairs channel, to C-Span, and across the continental United States. A warm hello also to the online audience watching this debate right now on MunkDebates.com. It's terrific to have you as virtual participants in tonight's proceedings. And hello to you, the over 3,000 people who have filled Roy Thomson Hall to capacity for yet another Munk Debate.

This evening we engage with the geopolitical debate of the moment: Has the administration of Barack Obama, through inaction and incompetence, as its critics will claim, fanned the flames of global conflict and encouraged the very forces that want to roll back individual rights, the rule of law, and economic globalization? Or — and it's a big "or" — has this president wisely and courageously disavowed the role of global policeman for the United States, a role embraced by his predecessor, in favour of alliance-building, and the limited, targeted use of military power? These, ladies and gentlemen, are the battle lines of tonight's contest.

The presence on the stage — in mere moments — of four outstanding debaters would not be possible without the public-spiritedness of our hosts this evening. Please join me in a warm round of appreciation for the co-founders of the Aurea Foundation and our hosts tonight, Peter and Melanie Munk.

Now for the moment we've been waiting for. Let's get our debaters out here on centre stage and our debate underway. Speaking first, for the motion, "Be it resolved: President Obama has emboldened our enemies and made the world a more dangerous place," is Robert Kagan, one of America's most prominent writers and thinkers on all things foreign policy, and the Brookings Institution's senior scholar. Joining Bob Kagan on the "pro" side of this debate is a Pulitzer Prize–winning writer, the international affairs columnist for the *Wall Street Journal*, and the former editor-in-chief of the *Jerusalem Post*, Bret Stephens.

Now, one great team of debaters deserves another, and I'd like you all to join me in welcoming a woman of singular accomplishment to the Munk Debates. She's a renowned scholar of international affairs, a former senior official in the U.S. State Department, and is currently CEO of the prestigious New America Foundation. Ladies and gentlemen, Anne-Marie Slaughter. Ms. Slaughter's debating partner tonight is no stranger to this series. Brain cell for brain cell, he is one of the most formidable debaters to appear on this stage. Please welcome bestselling author and the host of *Fareed Zakaria GPS*, CNN's flagship global affairs program, Fareed Zakaria.

Before we call on our debaters for their opening remarks, I need the help of all of you in this hall with a simple task: our countdown clock — my favourite part of these evenings. This clock will appear on the screen at various times of tonight's debate, including opening and closing statements, and for timed rebuttals. When you see it count down to zero please join me in a round of applause. This is going to keep our speakers on their toes, and our debate on schedule.

Now finally, let's find out how this audience voted on tonight's resolution, "Be it resolved: President Obama has emboldened our enemies and made the world a more dangerous place." The results are interesting: 43 percent of you agreed, and 57 percent disagreed. We have an almost tied vote! How did you answer our second question: Depending on what you hear tonight, are you open to changing your mind? Wow — 93 percent of you are flexible! This is a crowd that can be wooed and is very much open to what our debaters have to say. They clearly have their work cut out for them.

It's time for our opening statements. As per convention, the "pro" side will speak first. Bret Stephens, it was agreed that you would have the floor first. Your six minutes begins now.

BRET STEPHENS: Do you remember the first time? No, I don't mean *that* first time. I mean the first time you heard Barack Obama, the first time you were spellbound by his promises: we were going to defeat al Qaeda; we were going to win the war in Afghanistan while getting out of Iraq; we would reset relations with Russia; we would have a new beginning with the Muslim world and strengthen ties with our partners in Europe and the Americas; we would reassure allies in Asia, save the environment, stop Iran from getting the bomb, and prevent human rights atrocities and acts of genocide. This seems like a very long time ago, does it not?

Six years later, there is one thing we can say for sure: not one of those goals has been achieved. According to a RAND Corporation study, the number of jihadists more than doubled between 2010 and 2013, and that doesn't include the rise of ISIL. We are not out of Iraq, but back in Iraq. Relations with Russia have been reset to about 1956 levels. A Syrian dictator continues to gas his people with impunity, the only difference being that he switched from sarin to chlorine. Iran is far closer to a bomb today than it was when Obama took office. America is now more hated and distrusted in countries like Pakistan and Egypt than it was even when George W. Bush was president. And the war in Afghanistan, for which so many young Americans and young Canadians gave their lives, has not, to say the least, been won.

Some might say, "It isn't all Obama's fault. He's been dealt a tough hand. The world is a complicated place." Ladies and gentlemen, presidents are often dealt a tough hand. Roosevelt got a bad hand from Hoover; Reagan got a bad hand from Carter. What makes a good president is the ability to meet the goals he sets, define events more than he is defined by events, and leave the United States stronger and better respected in the world. This has not, to say the least, been the mark of Obama's tenure. Indeed, such is the gap between expectation and delivery that one might say, to paraphrase a famous line, that never in the field of political self-promotion have so many been promised so much by someone who delivered so little.

Why is this? I think there's a competence problem. Remember, this is the president who was busy calling ISIL the junior varsity team right up until ISIL took Mosul. This was the president who didn't bother finding out just who the National Security Agency (NSA) was wiretapping among our allies. But the larger problem is that this is a president who thinks that speeches are a substitute for action, a president who has compiled a record of being harsh with his allies in the world while going out of his way to accommodate America's adversaries. This is a president who talks about the importance of rules and then fails to enforce them.

"When dictators commit atrocities, they depend on the world to look the other way. If we fail to act, the Assad regime will see no reason to stop using chemical weapons, other tyrants will have no reason to think twice." That was Barack Obama explaining why the world had to punish Syria for its chemical weapons' use right before he explained why he wasn't going to punish Syria. As a result, America is no longer feared by its enemies, and we are no longer trusted by our friends.

Why is this uniquely dangerous? First, because perceptions shape actions: our enemies got the message that they can do whatever they want as long as they have the capability and the will to do so. "If the U.S. meets bullets with words, tyrants will draw their own conclusions" is not Dick Cheney talking. It's my colleague Anne-Marie Slaughter in an op-ed earlier this year. The second reason is that rogue regimes have an incentive to act sooner rather than later because they know Obama still has two years in office and might suspect that the next president will have more of a spine. The third reason is that if America's allies can't trust the United States, they will go their own way. There are dangerous rogues on this earth and equally dangerous freelancers.

This is a world of unprecedented volatility, at least in our lifetimes. Your enemies are tempted to strike and your allies are tempted to pre-empt, and all the while, as the global superpower, you are on the hook, even while you are losing control. Let me close by reminding you that Barack Obama won a Nobel Peace Prize in 2009, in the expectation of making the world a safer, better, and more peaceful place. As you follow our debate, ask yourself this question, with the benefit of hindsight: Would you still give him that prize? Thank you very much.

RUDYARD GRIFFITHS: Three seconds to spare, Bret, which is pretty impressive. Anne-Marie Slaughter, you are up next.

ANNE-MARIE SLAUGHTER: Blaming Barack Obama for the state that the world is in right now is like blaming a Caribbean island for a hurricane. Think very carefully about what our opponents have to prove. Not only do they have to prove that the world would be less dangerous if Barack Obama were not president, but they have to prove that the world is as dangerous as it is *because* he has emboldened our enemies. It is a two-step argument: they have to prove that Putin would not have annexed Crimea or invaded Ukraine, but for Obama's actions. Putin toughened after [Viktor] Yanukovych, the Ukrainian president, fled. At that moment, Putin's advisers were telling him that the United States sought only to overturn regimes. Putin got more serious; he didn't believe the United States was a threat. Only when he thought the Americans were more hard-line did Putin invade.

Or take ISIL. ISIL is not responding to Barack Obama's lack of action; ISIL is responding to the fact that Barack Obama refuses to pay ransoms and is bombing their troops. They are more likely to take action against us because of these moments. It is not because he has emboldened our enemies.

9

You've already heard that I am known for some criticisms of our president. I have disagreed with him strongly and strenuously on Syria. But my criticisms have not been that he emboldened Assad to take action. My main criticism is that once Assad decided, for his own good reasons, to obliterate the opposition, Obama could have been doing more to try to bring the parties to the peace table. To go back to my Caribbean island analogy, in the aftermath of a hurricane, you can certainly criticize the leaders of a country for not doing things to mitigate the damage or make it easier to rebuild, but you cannot blame them for the fact that the hurricane came in the first place.

I think Obama could have done different things in response to the recent crisis in Syria, but I don't think there's anything Obama could have done that would have stopped Assad from doing what he did. Assad wanted the Syrian conflict to be between his government and terrorists, and that is exactly what he got.

Now let's look at how Obama has actually worked to make the world a safer place. The single greatest threat that we face, which we also dealt with under George W. Bush, is the danger of a terrorist group with a nuclear weapon. Ending nuclear proliferation is absolutely essential. People such as Henry Kissinger, George Shultz [U.S. secretary of state under Ronald Reagan], Sam Nunn [current CEO of the Nuclear Threat Initiative], and Bill Perry [U.S. secretary of defense under Bill Clinton] all agree that halting nuclear proliferation is the single biggest achievement we have to work toward; otherwise, we risk facing a world with some ten, twenty, or thirty nuclear nations.

Barack Obama has worked doggedly for a deal with Iran. He's been extremely tough when he's needed to be; he's imposed sanctions; he's made clear that he will take no measures off the table; and he is closer now than anyone has been in twenty years to a deal with the country. We don't know if Obama will reach these targets, but if he does, it could reshape the entire region.

He has decimated al Qaeda, he took out Osama bin Laden, and he is working very hard and successfully to contain ISIL. He understands the difficulty of trying to eradicate the group and is working on something more tangible. He's also strengthened regional and international organizations. Contrary to what it looked like when he came into office, nobody now acts without the United Nations. He's re-established the rule of multilateralism at a time when it's very important to restrain China and Russia.

And those are just the state-to-state problems. What about the deeper problems? If you're reading the headlines today about why the world is such a dangerous place, you're not just reading about Russia or ISIL. You're reading about Ebola. You're reading about ungoverned spaces all over the world that give rise to disease, to violence, to wars that spill over borders and ultimately then fuel extremism of all kinds.

Solutions to these problems are slow and complicated; they can't be plotted out on a chessboard. But by focusing on issues like development, poverty eradication, and rebuilding governance we can move toward solving longer-term crises that we ultimately have to address: climate change — the thing that's causing those hurricanes in the Caribbean islands I've been talking about — is just one example. He's certainly done more work on these bigger issues than any president in the past few decades.

RUDYARD GRIFFITHS: Thank you, Anne-Marie. Bob Kagan, you're next with your opening statement. Please proceed, sir.

ROBERT KAGAN: Thank you all for coming out here tonight to listen to a debate about foreign policy. I'd like to think we could get as many Americans out for a night like this as Canadians we have here this evening — maybe some day. I know my colleagues are very pleased to be here. This is an excellent day to be defending Barack Obama — in Canada. I suspect it might be a little bit tougher back in the United States. We all saw the results of the election last night. Did you notice President Obama's approval ratings? What you may not know is that his general approval rating is significantly higher than his foreign policy approval rating.

His general approval rating among the American people is between 40 and 45 percent. His foreign policy approval rating is between 30 and 35 percent. That's George W. territory, folks. That's George W. in 2006. You Canadians may not trust the American people's judgement, and I would accept that. Maybe Americans are wrong now and maybe they were wrong in 2006 with George W. But maybe they were right both times — that's another possibility.

The other thing that is interesting with regard to this debate is that the American public, when asked, "Is the world a more dangerous place or has it gotten more dangerous in the last few years?" 65 percent say yes. They're not in any doubt. Are they wrong? Anne-Marie made a good point: there are two parts to this question. Is the world more dangerous, and does Barack Obama have anything to do with it?

I think the world clearly is more dangerous. Fareed, who has written some brilliant articles over the years, wrote one a few months ago saying that the world was actually in pretty good shape. Better than it had been for years. And he talked about statistics that Steven Pinker, the evolutionary psychologist at Harvard, came up with, noting that violence had declined. Pinker's explanation is that people have just gotten nicer. I have a different explanation. Pinker's study begins in 1945. Violence had declined from 1945 steadily over the decades. Why is that? What happened in 1945?

What happened in 1945 is that on the ruins of the greatest world catastrophe we had ever known, World War II, the democratic nations — the United States, Canada, the European nations, and Japan — got together and built a liberal world order that was strengthened over the decades and achieved three extraordinary things: one, an enormous spread of democracy; another, an enormous increase in prosperity, the likes of which we had never seen before; and finally, an end to great-power conflict of the kind we saw in the first part of the twentieth century.

If the world is more dangerous it is because that is what is at risk today. Now, I don't know what the future holds and maybe things will even out, but I see signs that this world order is at risk. One element is that we see that the number of democracies around the world has been declining steadily; we see what's happening to the global economy on balance; and now for the first time in Europe since 1945, we see cross-border aggression by one nation for the purpose of changing borders, something we thought we had eradicated in Europe.

Is all of this Barack Obama's fault? Of course not. Have Barack Obama's policies made these situations worse? Of course they have. We know how ISIL got to be what it is today. It was because the United States prematurely withdrew a limited number of troops from Iraq. It was because the president did not listen to Anne-Marie, who repeatedly said that if we can support a moderate opposition in Syria, we may be able to avoid having the vacuum filled by jihadists.

Well, lo and behold, the vacuum *has* been filled by jihadists, and Iraq *has* begun to fall apart. Are we supposed to believe that Barack Obama had nothing to do with any of this — that he's a Caribbean island sitting back and watching the hurricane go by? American presidents are not all-powerful, but they are not bereft of all power either.

In East Asia, we have a situation of increasing tension.

China is growing more aggressive, or at least wants to flex its elbows a little bit more. That's not Barack Obama's fault. But now we see Japan becoming increasingly independent, nationalist, and perhaps taking steps that, if we're not careful, could lead to a conflagration in East Asia. Why is Japan acting like this? I'll quote from Anne-Marie again: "Because Japan is wondering whether Barack Obama can be trusted. His unwillingness to use force in Syria after he said that he was going to use force echoed around the world and raised doubts among our allies about whether we can be relied upon." But my time is up, so more to come!

RUDYARD GRIFFITHS: Well done, Bob. The final opening statement goes to Fareed Zakaria. The floor is yours.

FAREED ZAKARIA: Thank you so much. Ladies and gentleman, I very much hope you will be convinced by Bob Kagan, because he is so persuaded by my colleague Anne-Marie Slaughter, and I trust that you will vote the way Anne-Marie Slaughter is voting in this resolution tonight. Clearly, she is a fountain of wisdom and good judgement!

Let me address the proposition very simply. What has happened to the United States's enemies? Enemy number one, Osama bin Laden, is dead, last time I checked. Al Qaeda, the organization that launched the 9/11 attacks, has been decimated to the point that it has been unable for years now to even pretend to launch any kind of major terror operation, or even a minor one. It used to plan terror attacks; now it releases video cassettes.

Enemy number two: Iran. How's Obama done on that front? We will hear fulminations from the other side; you will hear facts from ours. In 2006, people from Saudi Arabia, Egypt, and Jordan were polled on Iran's favourability ratings, and 75 percent of those who were asked gave Iran positive favourability ratings. Why? Because Iran was seen as the government standing up to the United States — the great aggressor, the imperial adventurer in the Middle East. In 2012, the same poll was done, and that statistic was down to 35 percent. Iran's favourability rating has dropped in half. Why? Barack Obama assembled an international coalition, put in place tough sanctions, gathered the Arabs together, and helped facilitate the unprecedented situation where the moderate Arab states are in alliance with Israel against Iran.

Russia has been the third great foe of the United States. The relationship between the two countries has been an interesting control experiment. Russia invaded a country during the Bush administration — Georgia. The consequence was zero. The Bush administration did absolutely nothing. George Bush was at the Olympics, spent some time palling around with Putin, and nothing happened. This year, when Russia did something similar, Barack Obama assembled a coalition of Western nations; NATO (the North Atlantic Treaty Organization) introduced tough sanctions; the European Union put real sanctions in place for the first time; and the United States implemented even tougher sanctions. In Russia right now growth has slowed to zero, its stock market has collapsed, the ruble is down 25 percent, and they've had to jack up interest rates — just yesterday they were up 150 basis points. If you're wondering where to park your cash, you can get 9.5 percent in Russia, but I still don't think any of you are going to do it.

Those are the three principal adversaries that the United States has faced during Obama's time in office, and I've highlighted what he's been able to accomplish. His administration has also been able to carry out a lot of pre-emptive moves. They have recognized that if the United States is going to play the kind of role Bob Kagan wants it to, as the guarantor of stability for the twenty-first century, Asia is the place where they'll need to take action. In about three years, three of the four largest economies in the world are all going to be in Asia. If the United States is going to be the superpower of the twenty-first century, which I believe it can be, it has to be a Pacific power. The Obama administration has zealously pursued a pivot to Asia, and it has been able to re-open American bases in the Philippines, something not even the sainted Ronald Reagan was able to do! He has been able to put in place a symbolic, but important, base of sorts in Australia. He has strengthened relations with Japan, making it clear that the disputed Senkaku Islands would be covered by the U.S. defence treaty. He has been able to offer a kind of vision of trade and opportunity to Asia that certainly President Bush was not able to do.

All of these things together have created a reality in which the United States *is* now much more able to play that role of balancer and stabilizer in Asia than it was before. It may not be enough. I, myself, would like the administration to do even more in this regard, but the basic strategy is correct. The core implementation has been done properly.

There's a final point I want to make about the world being so supposedly unstable. Clearly what we have is a world in which the Middle East is deeply unstable, but the rest of the world is in pretty good shape. And the Middle East, by the way, has been unstable for a while, in case you haven't noticed. Syria is the fourteenth country where the American military has intervened in the Islamic world since 1983, when Reagan sent Marines into Lebanon. How has that worked out for us in terms of stabilizing the situation there? Not so well. Bob Kagan tells us that things are terrible, that the world has become a much more dangerous place, and the American people are still figuring this out. He's been critical of many past presidents' foreign policy too: "The only word that describes [this] administration's policy is appeasement." He said that in 1999 about the Clinton administration. Or what about, "A future of American retreat and retrenchment is now certain" — Bob Kagan on the Bush administration before 9/11.

He now tells us that we are in the 1930s. But we are always in the 1930s according to Robert Kagan.

RUDYARD GRIFFITHS: Terrific opening statements. We certainly have a debate on our hands. Now we're going to do a quick round of rebuttals. We're going to have the "pro" side speak first, and Bob Kagan, you're up to respond.

ROBERT KAGAN: Fareed's right. I'm always worried that the world order we've created will collapse. I was worried in 1999. I was worried about what might happen in Iraq. I was nervous about terrorism, and some awful things did happen. I hope you appreciate the fact that I've been critical of both administrations, Republican and Democrat. I am worried that if we're not careful, we will, through lack of action, through misunderstanding, and through foolishness, lose control of a liberal order from which we've all benefited so much. And let me tell you, it is fragile.

Fareed thinks this liberal world order will go on forever. In his book *The Post-American World*, he said the liberal world order would continue even as the United States declines. And do you know why, according to Fareed? Because China will step up and uphold it. Because Russia will step up. Or India and Brazil. The rise of the rest! They'll come in and uphold the liberal world order even after the United States has lost the power.

I do worry about it. I don't want to ring incredible alarm bells, because I think we can overcome the situation that we're in right now. But the task that I have today is to ask the question as to whether Barack Obama's policies have taken a dangerous world and made it better or worse. If you listened to our colleagues here, you would think Barack Obama has accomplished miracles. If you listen to Anne-Marie carefully, she is suggesting that

Obama is *going* to prevent Iran from getting a nuclear weapon. Well, I'll take that on faith.

What about global warming? I'm really impressed by the incredible proposal that the United States, China, India, and Europe have finally come together to solve, or at least address, the problem of climate change. Maybe Obama will be able to do that in his last two years; he certainly was not able to do it in the previous six.

Look at his record of achievements: I'm thrilled that Osama bin Laden is dead; I think that's a great victory. I just wish we weren't in a situation like we are in now, where we're facing a terrorist organization that is trying to create its *own* state, which is much more complicated than dealing with individual terrorists operating in failed states. That is what ISIL is trying to achieve!

RUDYARD GRIFFITHS: Bret, we'll now have your rebuttal. Thank you.

BRET STEPHENS: Listening to Anne-Marie, I was reminded of *Life of Brian,* one of my favourite movies. If you've seen it, you'll remember the bitter disputes between the People's Front of Judea and the Judean People's Front. Anne-Marie and Fareed have told us that al Qaeda is decimated. And yet, Jabhat al-Nusra exists; we have al Qaeda in the Arabian Peninsula; we have al Qaeda nearly taking over the entire country of Mali, stopped only by a French intervention — an intervention the Obama administration initially opposed. And now we have ISIL, which, you're right, is not al Qaeda — it's more extreme than al Qaeda.

Nobody doubts the great tactical victory of killing Osama bin Laden. But I don't think any intelligent person here would dispute the idea that al Qaeda and jihadist groups that threaten us here and our interests both in the Middle East and around the world are more powerful today than they used to be.

Now another movie that I'm very fond of, and I'm sure is dear to all your hearts, too, is *Austin Powers*. You've heard Fareed talk about the sanctions that have decimated the Russian economy. As a matter of fact, the Russian economy has mainly been decimated by the fall in oil prices, which has been happening since June — a remarkable contraction, thanks largely to the great energy revolution that is taking place here in Canada as well as in the United States. A story in the *Wall Street Journal* just a few days ago outlined the effects of sanctions on Vladimir Putin's favourite bank. It said that after sanctions this bank has lost nearly $21 million. Do you remember that scene in *Austin Powers* where Dr. Evil says, "We will make a ransom of $1 million?" Twenty-one million dollars is pocket change for any Russian oligarch, but is being trumpeted as a great achievement.

Anne-Marie mentioned nuclear proliferation and what President Obama has done to stop it. What is she talking about? North Korea may be on the eve of another nuclear test. The Saudi Arabians come to our office regularly and threaten to develop or purchase nuclear weapons if Iran gets closer to a bomb. In 2008 Iran had 3,900 centrifuges and today it has 19,000. Admittedly, they're frozen, but we will see how long that lasts. So I think it is a little early to trumpet that achievement.

Lastly, Fareed told us about the pivot to Asia. A 2013 story in Reuters noted that three years after the pivot was announced there were zero troops in Australia. The Trans-Pacific Partnership (TPP) agenda is dead. I'd love these achievements — if they were real.

RUDYARD GRIFFITHS: The important facts of this debate are certainly emerging quick and fast. Ms. Slaughter, you are up next with your rebuttal.

ANNE-MARIE SLAUGHTER: So, we have definitely established one thing without any question. Barack Obama has emboldened the Republican Party!

Our opponents are witty and are deftly using my own quotes against me, but I want to remind you what *they* have to prove. They have to prove that the world is more dangerous now than it would be if Barack Obama were not president — which is heavily counterfactual — and that one of the major reasons we got here is that he emboldened our enemies. What we've heard is that he has not achieved all the goals he laid out in 2009 — and that is not exactly unique to Barack Obama. It is pretty much standard for politicians. He had high hopes; he did not achieve them. We have heard that he is not Ronald Reagan or Franklin Delano Roosevelt. I'll accept that.

The opposition has said he is not competent; he gives speeches instead of creating good policy. What we haven't heard is how any of that emboldened our enemies and led to the world becoming a more dangerous place than it would be if he were not president. You can like him or not like him. You can think he gives too many speeches and he doesn't take action, but our opponents have to show that it is his inaction or action that makes the world worse off.

Bret and Bob are also attacking the good things that both Fareed and I say Obama has done. Perhaps he has not yet achieved a deal with Iran — and he may not before his term is up — but he has done more than any other president has on this issue. Our opponents agree that a deal is absolutely central to avoiding nuclear proliferation in the Middle East because if Iran gets a nuclear weapon, Saudi Arabia will also get a nuclear weapon, and then Turkey and Egypt will want to get them too. Those are the stakes Obama is playing for.

The worst thing the other side has said, which was actually quoting me against me, is that Obama may have made the Japanese government nervous. I understand how they interpreted my words, but as far as I know we are doing quite well with Japan. TPP is not dead yet. Let's see how it unfolds with a Republican congress. And frankly, if Obama did make the government of Japan nervous by not following through on his threatened strikes against Assad, it was because he reasoned that leaving chemical weapons in Syria, where ISIL or any other group could get a hold of them, would have been a worse threat.

RUDYARD GRIFFITHS: Fareed, we're going to give you the final rebuttal. Three minutes are up on the clock.

FAREED ZAKARIA: We have to try and figure out a central premise tonight: Is the world deep, dark, dangerous, and disordered or are we in pretty good shape? And Bob Kagan correctly quoted me as saying I think the world is in pretty good shape. If you look at other parts of the globe and don't simply analyze the crisis du jour, and the bomb du jour, and the execution du jour in the Middle East, what you see, for example, is a renewed Latin America. Thirty years ago the continent was ruled by dictators, had economies that were run in quasi-socialist fashion and were deeply anti-American and anti-Western. Today Latin America is a transformed continent — democracies are everywhere — with the exceptions of Cuba, Venezuela, and Bolivia. For the most part, there is a free-market orientation. It is quite remarkable how much anti-Americanism has waned.

I interviewed the new president of Mexico, who comes from the Institutional Revolutionary Party (PRI), historically a deeply anti-American political party, and he remarked how extraordinary it was that the PRI has transformed into a party that is fundamentally pro-American. You can see similar things happening across the continent. Go to Asia and you'll see a different continent from thirty years ago. Think of the Asia of the 1970s with Mao and revolutionary guerrilla movements, with India and its pro-Soviet stance. All of that has been completely transformed. India recently elected a new pro-growth, pro-American prime minister. Indonesia had a similar experience; Japan a somewhat similar experience. Look at Africa compared to thirty years ago. In all these places there are extraordinary opportunities.

It turns out we often ask people around the world what they think of the American president. When asked, "How much confidence do you have in the U.S. president?" in the last year of the Bush administration, the Germans said 14 percent; in 2014, that number is 71 percent. In France: 13 percent under Bush, 83 percent under Obama. In Indonesia: 23 percent under Bush, 60 percent under Obama. In Israel: 57 percent under Bush, 71 percent under Obama. In China: 30 percent under Bush, 51 percent under Obama. I could go on all night. It's a long list of countries, but I will close with one near and dear to your hearts. In Canada: 27 percent approval rating in 2007, and an 81 percent approval rating for Obama in 2013.

RUDYARD GRIFFITHS: Wow! The table has certainly been set by our opening statements and our rebuttals, and now we have an opportunity to get these two teams of debaters engaged with each other directly. Bob, I'm going to start with you. Fareed brought up an interesting statistic: fourteen interventions in the Middle East since the Marines went into Lebanon. Why do you think that *more* intervention would have made the world a safer place when the record itself looks atrocious?

ROBERT KAGAN: First of all, the president *has* chosen more intervention, so he obviously thinks it's the right thing to do; Anne-Marie thinks it's the right thing to do. The problem is that in this case Obama has ignored the advice of his own hand-picked chairman of the Joint Chiefs of Staff — a general of the armed forces — about how to carry out U.S. involvement in the Middle East. You know, you could make a list of all the things that have gone wrong in American foreign policy over the years, but the question is: Has the long thrust of American foreign policy produced a better world? And I doubt anyone who is up here on this stage would disagree that what has been accomplished since 1945 has been extraordinary, despite all the mistakes.

I want to respond to one of Anne-Marie's and Fareed's central points: I understand that Anne-Marie wants us to say that Barack Obama has done worse than some other president, and that Fareed wants us to prove that Barack Obama has done a worse job than George Bush. But unfortunately, that's not the question we're being asked. I would agree George W. Bush did a lot of things wrong, but in the context of the question "Has Barack Obama made things better or worse, given the state of the world?" the opposition has not provided any facts on how Obama has made things better — they've merely identified what they *hoped* he could achieve.

RUDYARD GRIFFITHS: Anne-Marie, give us something specific, something that Barack Obama has done up to this point in his presidency that you think has improved the global climate.

ANNE-MARIE SLAUGHTER: He has turned to Asia and strengthened all of our alliances with the continent, particularly with Southeast Asia. We are actively present in Asia in a way that George Bush was not. Bob said he is worried that the world order that the United States, Canada, and all the allies in World War II built is at risk, but George W. Bush did more to disturb that system with his invasion of Iraq, against the will of the Security Council and pretty much the world, than anyone else. Barack Obama has systematically rebuilt the trust of the world through our willingness to use the Security Council and other institutions.

ROBERT KAGAN: That's just nonsense, Anne-Marie. First of all, everyone in the audience tonight should know that all the debaters on this stage supported the Iraq war.

In terms of Obama systematically rebuilding? You must not talk to anyone in the world, including our allies, in order to believe that. If you talk to Japanese officials, they are worried about the extent of America's commitment to global leadership. Officials in Saudi Arabia, in the UAE [United Arab Emirates], in Israel, are also worried. Radosław Sikorski, the Polish foreign minister, said the American guarantee is now worthless.

BRET STEPHENS: No, he said something worse.

ROBERT KAGAN: He said something worse? What did he say?

BRET STEPHENS: He said it's bullshit.

ROBERT KAGAN: Oh, I don't like to use that kind of language in a friendly debate!

RUDYARD GRIFFITHS: Fareed, I want to hear your opinion on this.

FAREED ZAKARIA: This is one of the things that Dick Cheney has been saying for a while — that when he goes abroad all his friends tell him that the United States can't be trusted. And of course that is true. The corpulent monarchs of Saudi Arabia and the United Arab Emirates who have lived fat off the hog from U.S. security are terrified that we are going to ask them to protect themselves, so they've sent in a few fighter planes to fight ISIL, tugging at our coattails for the most part. A certain number of senior officials in these places that had cosy relations with the past administrations feel that way.

Let's look at Japan, if I may, since you brought it up. About 20 percent of people living there trusted the U.S. president under Bush, 60 percent under Barack Obama. So, you can pull these arguments out of your hat when you say "the world has lost faith in Obama," but we actually have very good data that reveals the opposite. What would you like to see instead? Well, the one administration that Bob had almost no objections to was the Bush administration and —

ROBERT KAGAN: I had almost no objections to the Bush administration? I had the same objections you had, Fareed!

FAREED ZAKARIA: In the context of the Iraq war. But you loved the aggressiveness, expansionism, and the hegemony. Bob's problem with the Syrian intervention is that it is not vigorous enough. He wants Obama to do it more wholeheartedly, with lots of troops, and maybe ground forces, like we did in Iraq, which worked out so well.

Yes, I was one of the people who originally thought that getting rid of Saddam Hussein was a good idea. But with $2 trillion, 175,000 troops, 5,000 troops dead, and 400,000 Iraqis perhaps dead and wounded later, I learned something, and I don't want to replicate that lesson in Syria, the neighbouring country.

BRET STEPHENS: Our opponents would like nothing more than to make this debate a referendum on the Bush administration. You notice how we've somehow slowly worked our way into a conversation about Bush.

Now, when it comes to military intervention, again, I would love to just quote a little piece here from Anne-Marie, because it's so wonderful. She was typecast on your side of the debate, but she has a kind of split personality here and I'm just bringing out the hawkish side of her. She talked about how the United States "together with as many countries as will co-operate, could use force to eliminate Syria's fixed-wing aircraft as a first step toward enforcing Resolution 2139. Aerial bombardment would still likely continue via helicopter, but such a strike would announce immediately that the game has changed. After the strike, the U.S., France, and Britain should ask the Security Council's approval of the action taken, as they did after NATO's intervention in Kosovo." So she's suggesting that they get post facto legitimation of the military strike, the hard military strike that you wanted to carry out against the Assad regime. And I couldn't agree with you more, Anne-Marie.

Interesting story in a Japanese newspaper not too long ago: it noted that because of military cuts in the United States, we will have a four-month stretch next year where there is no U.S. aircraft carrier in the western Pacific. Why is Japan building a nuclear plutonium facility for $21 billion that will produce nine tonnes of weapons-usable plutonium a year if they are not having serious doubts about the reliability of Barack Obama's security guarantees?

RUDYARD GRIFFITHS: The question was directed to Anne-Marie, so you respond first, and then, Fareed, you get a follow-up.

ANNE-MARIE SLAUGHTER: So, I will be completely frank. When I was originally asked to be on this side of this debate, I did wonder if it was the right choice. Because I have been very, very vocal, as you've heard, in terms of what I think the Obama administration should have done in Syria. And I don't think that they responded correctly. But then I thought, "Wait a minute, I disagree with this president on a number of issues, but do I actually think he's made the world more dangerous? No, I don't." In the first place, most of the things we're describing, like China rising, which is why Japan is really nervous, are happening completely independently of Barack Obama. The question is: What does he do in response? And I value that he at least *tries* to get a trade agreement, which is certainly more than any other president —

BRET STEPHENS: He doesn't try.

ANNE-MARIE SLAUGHTER: Yes, he does. He launched the TPP and the Transatlantic Trade and Investment Partnership (TTIP) in Europe.

BRET STEPHENS: When was the last time Barack Obama gave a major foreign policy address, where he outlined something along the lines of what Bill Clinton did with the North American Free Trade Agreement (NAFTA)? He simply has not. We all have this fantasy about Barack Obama: he was the saviour — this Jesus! We had the feeling, but it didn't work out.

FAREED ZAKARIA: Bret is now sounding like the college Republican at the cocktail party that you're trying to get out of conversation with.

By the way, I have a reading suggestion for you if you're enjoying this debate. Bret has a new book out; it's called *America in Retreat: The New Isolationism and the Coming Global Disorder*. It's wonderfully written, vivid, and it has all the things you look for in a good work of fiction. I really suggest that you pick it up on your next long beach vacation.

Let's try to broaden this topic. Foreign policy is surely also about rebuilding American strength. I think all of us would agree that the only way the United States can play the pivotal role that we want it to is for the country to be fundamentally strong at home, particularly economically. How did the United States do coming out of the Great Recession compared to Europe and Japan? The Obama administration, in co-ordination with the federal reserve, had an aggressive monetary response, an aggressive fiscal response, and an aggressive regulatory response, by which I mean that the banks were given stress tests until we basically made them more like Canadian banks. The three things worked brilliantly. The United States is the strongest economy out of this Great Recession — no question. You ask any economist in the world to judge the performance of those three blocs, and it is clear that because of public policy, the United States has come out of the global financial crisis in much better shape. It has also done well because of other public policies where again the Obama administration deserves some credit: fracking, for example.

But those successes aside, Europe is disunited, dysfunctional, and now tripping into its third recession; Japan continues to simply try monetary stimulus because it doesn't have the guts to do the other hard things that it has to do to achieve economic viability; but the United States is demographically and economically succeeding, and this vibrancy will allow the country to power itself forward.

ROBERT KAGAN: Does this mean it isn't the post-American world anymore?

FAREED ZAKARIA: I said in the book that the United States was going to be the most powerful country in the twenty-first century by far. The question we have to ask ourselves is: Are we strengthened by more interventions? And I would tell you that one of the things that Obama deserves a lot of credit for is being somewhat restrained in terms of the foolish and misguided adventurism that has taken place in the past. He's taken a page from Dwight Eisenhower. Eisenhower was asked by the French, the British, and the Israelis to intervene in Suez. He refused. He was asked by the French to intervene in Dien Bien Phu. He refused. He was asked by the Taiwanese twice during the Formosa Straits crisis to intervene and he said no. At the time, people like Bob Kagan and Bret Stephens pilloried Eisenhower. But the reality was that these were very wise exercises in restraint. Sometimes, as those of you in business know, saying no is the hardest thing to do. And Obama has said no in many, many important cases.

ROBERT KAGAN: And by the way, the effect of Eisenhower's policies in 1956 was to cut the legs out from all of our allies, which I am sure you know perfectly well, Fareed, from your historical knowledge. I hesitate to keep quoting

Anne-Marie, but here's what I really think. I think this has all been quite unfair. We have basically been asking Fareed to essentially hold up this argument all by himself, since —

FAREED ZAKARIA: I'm doing fine!

ROBERT KAGAN: Since effectively Anne-Marie should have been on our side, as she originally thought. Let me read you something that Anne-Marie wrote in April 2014: "The solution to the crisis in Ukraine lies in part in Syria. It is time for U.S. President Barack Obama to demonstrate that he can order the offensive use of force in circumstances other than secret drone attacks or covert operations. The result will change the strategic calculus not only in Damascus, but also in Moscow, not to mention Beijing and Tokyo." Another statement that —

FAREED ZAKARIA: Obama is doing it now, so Putin must be trembling. Obama has now done four or five hundred strikes in Syria. Let's see whether the world starts quaking.

ROBERT KAGAN: Let's talk about something for a second. We've been talking about Putin, and Anne-Marie is exactly right. Putin went into Crimea because of what happened to Yanukovych in Ukraine. What about since then? The point of Anne-Marie's piece about Syria was: How do you deter Putin from going further than he's already gone? Fareed is talking about all the incredible suffering that the Russian economy is going through, which is certainly true. The only problem is that Putin continues to pour weapons and troops into Ukraine every day — in violation of his own agreements — and the West's only response is, "We'll think about more sanctions in a few weeks." We couldn't be bothered to provide the Ukrainians with some weaponry and training, and some capacity to defend themselves! It is the least we could have done to help Ukraine. We didn't need to intervene, or put troops on the ground —

RUDYARD GRIFFITHS: Let's stop for a second here. I'm not doing any work tonight and I love that. You are all doing a fabulous job, but I think Anne-Marie has the right to respond to Bob. Anne-Marie, do you think the Obama administration's response to Putin's aggression has been sufficient?

ANNE-MARIE SLAUGHTER: Yes. But regarding Syria, I knew Bob would quote that against me and I did believe those things when I wrote them. I absolutely thought it was critical in terms of sending a message to Putin. I spent half the summer talking to Russian experts about what drives Putin and I absolutely think at this point that, had we done what I was suggesting, it wouldn't have changed Putin's calculus.

BRET STEPHENS: So don't do what she's suggesting now. Six months from now it'll be another different story.

ANNE-MARIE SLAUGHTER: But, equally importantly, it might well have torpedoed our negotiations with Iran. As much as I believe that we should be acting differently in Syria, I fully understand Barack Obama's rationale. He believes a deal with Iran is the single most important goal in the region, and he's not going to do anything that strengthens Iranian hardliners and jeopardizes it. I might make a different decision in his position, but I respect it as a foreign policy calculation that is absolutely focused on an extremely dangerous threat. I don't believe he is enticing Putin to do things that Putin wouldn't otherwise do. And he may well be working toward what is the biggest foreign policy success of all.

BRET STEPHENS: Can I take a step back and make a clarification, because Fareed said something that was very hurtful to me and also, quite frankly, hypocritical. *I* was certainly no college Republican — I voted for Bill Clinton in my first election. *Fareed* was the head of the party of the right at Yale. *He's* the college Republican!

More substantively, when we talk about Ukraine, Syria, and Iraq we're talking about interventions. Let's be intelligent adults here. There are some interventions that work and there are some interventions that fail. As a leader, you have to be pragmatic, prudential, and think things through. Every president should do that when confronted with various crises.

Now let's apply that reasoning to Syria. For the first six months of the Syrian uprising, when we failed to lift a finger, it was an almost entirely peaceful uprising of

Syrian citizens saying "enough" to tyranny. It was an effort to replicate what happened in Tahrir Square in Egypt, which had inspired the world. The Free Syrian Army only started to form as a response to massive brutality by the Assad regime.

We refused to support the Free Syrian Army because the administration didn't think we knew enough about the rebels. And Obama liked to say that he was the man who ended wars, not started them. So things got worse. Next thing you know, there are 10,000, 50,000, 100,000, *200,000* people slaughtered. Obama still did nothing. Then 1,000 people were killed in a sarin gas attack and Obama's administration decided to make that their red line. We got involved in a lot of chemical weapon removal in Syria; however, we didn't remove them all, according to the UN organization and the NGO that is responsible for them. In the meantime, the tragedy of the Syrian people — while we have not intervened — has been extended to a million refugees in Jordan and the security of Jordan as a state. There are another million refugees in Lebanon; two million in Turkey. The crisis in Syria facilitated the rise of ISIL and caused the near collapse of the Iraqi state.

This has been the price of non-intervention. It's very easy for Fareed to say that interventions are very dangerous and have consequences — he's right. But there are consequences for non-intervention. Do yourselves a favour and look at pictures of Syrians who were starved to death by the Assad regime while we sat on our hands and talked about the difficulties of any kind of intervention. Syria has gone from a local crisis to an international catastrophe because we wouldn't get involved.

RUDYARD GRIFFITHS: I have to be conscious of the time. Fareed, you're going to have the last word in this section of the debate and then we're going to move into closing statements.

FAREED ZAKARIA: I think it is a fundamental misreading of Syria to look at it as a tale of democrats rising up against a dictatorial regime and us being unable to support them. Syria is really the third of the three great minority regimes that have existed in the Middle East. The first was the Christians in Lebanon. In the 1970s, we began to see a mass uprising against that minority regime, which turned into a brutal fifteen-year civil war, with one out of every twenty Lebanese killed. War-weary, they came to a power-sharing deal, which has held in fragile ways, but it has held.

Iraq was the second great minority regime of the Middle East. We kindly got rid of the Sunni minority, but they fought back an insurgency that continues to this day. Iraq is still the second-most violent country in the world, and the civil war has had huge consequences.

Syria is the third of these minority regimes, with the Alawites, who are 12 percent of the population, ruling over the Sunnis, who are 85 percent of the population. We are witnessing that power rebalancing take place. Assad's father, Hafez al-Assad, was an Alawite who brutally suppressed the Sunnis, and that opposition movement became violent and highly religious from the 1980s onward. Remember the Hama massacre, which took place twenty-five years ago? This situation has bubbled up again and we are now witnessing the result of it. So when we think about getting involved in this civil war, we in America need to be sure that: a) there are good guys in the country somewhere; b) we know who they are; c) we can find them, support them, and know they will win; and d) they will set up a Jeffersonian democracy at the end of this whole process. I think that the chances of that happening and our ability to make this happen by remote control are limited.

I met with the head of the political wing of the Free Syrian Army two years ago in Istanbul. He was a lovely man who talked about an open, pluralistic Syria in which everyone would participate. It was really heartening to hear him say that. Then I asked him, "When were you last in Syria?" And he said, "Not for a while. Thirty-one years ago." I said, "Where do you live now?" He said, "Stockholm." I said, "What do you do there?" He said, "I teach philosophy at the university." He's a Kant scholar, a very good one, I gather. That's the problem with the moderate Syrians. It's not that they are not moderate — it's that they are not really Syrian. The current head of the Syrian opposition has not been in Syria for twenty-four years.

ROBERT KAGAN: Can I just say one thing? The basic point that you're making, Fareed, is a point that has been made many times, and it is that if the Syrians are getting killed, it is their own damn fault and it's not our problem or our business. I can't tell you how many times this argument has been made throughout history.

FAREED ZAKARIA: No, Bob, I can give you a wonderful example of how we've helped. If we'd had a lot of troops there, we could establish some order and try to help create and support a moderate government of "good guys." Well, we did that in Iraq, right? We had 175,000 troops, we supported the government there, and we thought we had political stability and power-sharing deals. And here's what happened in Iraq — two-and-a-half million people fled Iraq never to return; 200,000 to 300,000 thousand civilians died; Christian life in Iraq, which had been in existence since the Bible, has essentially been extinguished. Roughly 500,000 Christians have fled Iraq, and all of that happened while we were occupying the country. So now we're sure that the solution to Syria's problems is for the United States to intervene? And I only ask you: Don't we ever learn something from those pictures of the Iraqis who have been killed, maimed, wounded, dispossessed, in large part *because* of the misadventures of American interventionism?

RUDYARD GRIFFITHS: We're now going to move to closing statements. Anne-Marie, you are going to go first with three minutes on the clock, starting now.

ANNE-MARIE SLAUGHTER: Debates are funny and witty, and we've heard lots of repartee and had lots of laughs. But there are actually some very serious issues at stake here. I agree more with Bret on Syria than I do with Fareed, but Fareed and I have debated this issue repeatedly and there's no certainty on it. As Fareed said, if we intervene in Syria, we might well end up with a situation like an Iraq or we could end up at war directly with Iran. I understand the arguments on both sides — either you make a prudent decision that you don't want to take that risk, or you decide to try because you believe in the end it *may* make a positive difference for the Syrian people.

Our opponents have an old-fashioned view of history — a great-man vision of history — whereby presidents and prime ministers single-handedly alter world events. For example, Kaiser Wilhelm was instrumental in starting World War I after Bismarck died; Neville Chamberlain could have stopped Hitler had he not agreed to a policy of appeasement; or Ronald Reagan ended the Cold War by defeating Gorbachev. I'm not sure that was ever an honest account of history, but I am very sure it does not apply today. We are no longer living in a world where you can plot out moves statesman to statesman like on a chessboard. We are in an extraordinarily complex world, a world in which we have governments, individuals, networks, and corporations all jumbled together in ways that make it almost impossible to predict what is going to happen if you make a decision.

In this world order, Barack Obama is playing a prudent hand. He knows he might be able to deter Putin, but he could also put the world at the brink of nuclear war. I do not think you can blame him for making the world more dangerous because he has decided not to risk nuclear war — or to risk war with Iran — in the Middle East. You can say he may not have made the world a safer place, or as safe a place as he would have liked, but I don't think you can charge him with having brought about the dangers that we find ourselves in because *he* has emboldened our enemies. Thank you.

RUDYARD GRIFFITHS: Concise and powerful closing statement. Bob Kagan, you're up next.

ROBERT KAGAN: Look, I'm not going to quote Anne-Marie now, but I *am* going to quote some other people: "When the president of the United States draws a red line, the credibility of his country is dependent on him backing up his word." Who said that? Leon Panetta, former secretary of defense under President Obama. Here's another quote: "I think when we stepped out of Iraq, in many ways, we created this vacuum in which not a lot of attention was paid to what was happening in Iraq or what was happening in Syria with the extremists who were developing a base of operations there. That combination, I think, is what produced the ISIL that we're confronting today," Leon Panetta again. Or how about, "Great nations need organizing principles, and 'don't do stupid stuff' is not an organizing principle." That was Hillary Clinton.

I could go on and on. But an extraordinary thing

has happened over the course of the Obama administration. Senior officials, cabinet officials — Bob Gates, effectively a non-partisan government servant who served presidents going back to Nixon, and Obama's former secretary of defense; Leon Panetta, a long-time Democrat in the House who was previously secretary of defense; Hillary Clinton, not anyone's idea of a college Republican, and former secretary of state; civil servants, foreign service officers like Robert Ford and Frederick Hough, who were the Syria experts for the Obama administration — all did something extraordinary when they left the administration. They really laid out some very serious critiques of how President Obama handled foreign policy. They were accused of disloyalty, but I don't know how you could accuse Leon Panetta or Hillary Clinton of disloyalty. They all effectively criticized, in very strong terms, President Obama's leadership. What explains that?

They believe the United States could play a better and more effective role in the world and they were willing to come out and criticize their own president in order to make that point. Listen to them more than you listen to us.

RUDYARD GRIFFITHS: Fareed, your closing statement, please. Three minutes are up on the clock.

FAREED ZAKARIA: We've all had a lot of fun, and it's been a great pleasure — I've been outed as a college Republican — though I wasn't ever a Republican because I wasn't a citizen of the United States in those days. But I will admit that's a legalism.

I want to just reiterate something that Anne-Marie said, which is important. Robert Kagan and Bret Stephens want a world that is stable, peaceful, prosperous, and that is undergirded by American power. This is a world that we all believe has been vastly beneficial for the United States, Canada, Europe, and by and large for the whole world. It has allowed the rise of Asia; it has allowed the transformation I spoke about in Latin America. But what has made that possible?

I would argue we can thank Franklin Roosevelt for it. After winning decisively in World War II, he decided to create the United Nations, an institution in which all countries would be represented, and which tried to make a systematic and institutionalized effort to produce a new kind of global politics that allowed all countries to be heard. And that is really what the United States, at its core, has been trying to do since 1945. The United States hasn't helped secure global order because it has gone into lots of third world countries, intervened, beaten up people, and killed leaders; it is because the United States has promoted a positive vision of building institutions of peace and prosperity that it has been able to preside over this world.

A crucial part of that role has been to exercise an element of restraint. The United States cannot use its awesome powers to get its way on everything — they must do things multilaterally, and try to find ways to do things diplomatically rather than militarily. This has been so much a part of the American foreign policy tradition. Yes, the United States has intervened unsuccessfully in some places — and it is not clear to me that sending half a million troops into Vietnam really upheld the global order. But it is so obvious to me that creating the UN, the World Bank, the IMF [International Monetary Fund], the Bretton Woods system, the World Trade Organization — all of those institutions — has been a crucial part of that liberal international tradition.

And Obama has been part of it. It is that kind of restraint, that kind of sober-minded, sensible, intelligent foreign policy that Obama represents. So I guess what I'm telling you is that he's sort of a closet Canadian. Vote for him, for God's sake.

RUDYARD GRIFFITHS: Bret Stephens, you're going to get the final word in this epic debate.

BRET STEPHENS: Last I checked, Canadian CF-18s were bravely joining coalition forces to bomb ISIL, and I commend Canada for being such a core member of a Western alliance which has upheld peace, prosperity, and freedom for the past seventy years.

Now, Fareed, you mentioned my book, and I'm glad you are enjoying it so much. I want to talk a little bit about what my book is about, because what is clear to us here is that the United States needs to find a Goldilocks recipe between the excess of idealism, which typified, say, Johnson in Vietnam or George W. Bush in Iraq — trying to be the world's priest, to change hearts, to

45

save souls, to make the world safe for democracy, that Wilsonian tradition — and what I would call the cold-hearted realism and the timidity that has typified the Obama administration.

You've heard a wonderful universe described today — a peaceful world where our only problems are in the Middle East. But there's also that little issue of Ukraine — who cares about that? — and same with air defence identification zones in the South China Sea. It's a scary world. So how do we chart a course between the Bush excesses and the lack of imagination, vision, courage, and initiative that I think has typified the Obama administration? Well that's what my book is about.

Now, something amazing happened in America in the last twenty-five years: our crime and murder rates, which were so staggeringly high in the 1970s and 1980s, went down. They went down because American police departments adopted what was known as broken-windows policing. They observed that if a single window is broken in a neighbourhood it's a sign that nobody's in charge, and so that window acts as an invitation to break all the rest of the windows to create disorder. Disorder and criminality aren't just causal; they're environmental.

I believe something like that is happening in the world, too. There were no consequences for Assad in Syria, no real consequences for Putin in Georgia or Ukraine; and the rogues of the world sensed that we now live in a place where no one is in charge, where the United States is afraid to intervene in all circumstances, which allows them to do whatever they want. We're entering into a broken-windows world. We need a foreign policy that understands that the role of a great power is to maintain order as a policeman, not as a priest — to be the man on the corner who is reassuring the good, deterring the tempted, and punishing the wicked. I look forward to a president who does that. Thank you.

RUDYARD GRIFFITHS: Strong closing statements from all. And to the debaters — wow, what a meaty, significant, and important debate we've had tonight. This is our fourteenth consecutive debate to a huge crowd here in Toronto. As always, Peter and Melanie Munk, thank you. And thank you to our wonderful debaters.

Now the pièce de résistance of the evening is the second audience vote. Before you leave tonight, we're going to review how you voted earlier in the evening. I call it a split house: 43 percent in favour of the resolution to 57 percent against it — and the percentage that would change their minds is sky-high. I've never seen that before here. This room is really in play tonight and the final outcome, ladies and gentlemen, is in your hands. There's a ballot in your program. Ladies and gentlemen, thanks for a great debate.

Summary: The pre-debate vote was 43 percent in favour of the resolution and 57 percent against it. The final vote showed 32 percent in favour of the motion and 68 percent against. Given that more of the voters shifted to the team against the resolution, the victory goes to Anne-Marie Slaughter and Fareed Zakaria.

Pre-Debate Interviews
with Rudyard Griffiths

FAREED ZAKARIA IN CONVERSATION
WITH RUDYARD GRIFFITHS

RUDYARD GRIFFITHS: Ladies and gentlemen, we're back with Fareed Zakaria, the host of *Fareed Zakaria GPS*, CNN's flagship global affairs show, bestselling author, and journalist. Fareed, great to have you here in Toronto.

You've previously described Barack Obama as Henry Kissinger with a conscience, in terms of his foreign policy. Unpack that for us. What were you getting at?

FAREED ZAKARIA: And now I'm here today to not quite defend Barack Obama but to demonstrate the complexity of the real Obama. He's generally been able to do what he wants and not get caught in a situation where he's forced to commit major U.S. forces or the country to a foreign policy intervention that he doesn't believe is in America's national interest.

He has a kind of core realist criteria by which he

judges foreign policy. He's often said that he most admires George Bush Sr.'s foreign policy. He speaks admiringly of Kissinger. And his policy in the Middle East, for example, has been very realist. He's very tough on al Qaeda. He's not particularly interested in nation-building — he believes that's a fool's errand. So that kind of discipline, which I associate with Kissinger or Eisenhower, the ability to say no when there is a clamour for you to do something, is really quintessentially realist. And that's what I mean by the Kissinger part.

But there are a number of people in the media environment and perhaps a number of people within his White House who don't quite feel that way: Samantha Power, for example, his UN ambassador, who's written a whole book about the problem of genocide and actively wants the United States to do more. Clearly that tugs on Barack Obama's conscience, because every now and then you'll notice that, while maintaining this core realist foreign policy, he will make a few remarks that suggest that his heart is deeply moved and he wants to do something more interventionist; he'll say Assad must go and the use of chemical weapons would be America's red line — that ISIL will be destroyed.

And then I think to myself, "But doesn't the Barack Obama who has been so disciplined realize that we don't have a strategy to get Assad to go?" It's not entirely clear how we'd do it. If we were to pursue this policy we would have to confront the same issue we had in Iraq, which is how to govern a complex multi-ethnic, multi-sectarian society. Obama understands that but he can't stop himself from making those remarks. He can't stop himself from signalling that he's not just Kissinger. And that's what I mean by calling him Kissinger with a conscience.

But it's a bad idea. He has to be one or the other. He can't make casual statements that suggest humanitarian sympathy, because he's the president of the United States. As a columnist, I can say Assad should go, but if Obama says it, the United States better have a foreign policy and a strategy that is going to oust that leader. While I think it is reflective of an honourable part of Barack Obama — that he has a conscience — it doesn't lead to the best foreign policy.

RUDYARD GRIFFITHS: Bret Stephens and Bob Kagan are no doubt going to argue tonight that some of those missteps — erasing red lines, for example — directly cause the aggression we see from leaders like Vladimir Putin, or possible future aggression on the part of the Chinese. Do you buy that argument? Is this president perceived as weak internationally, and has this caused anxiety amongst allies and emboldened our enemies?

FAREED ZAKARIA: No, it's fundamentally nonsense, quite frankly. First of all, it's great to show students what deters countries, but very few people sit and watch what you're doing in country X 5,000 miles away and infer that in a very different situation in country Y you would do something similar. Leaders understand that international relations are highly contextual — the fact that the United States sent 500,000 troops into Vietnam doesn't mean it will send 500,000 troops into Russia next year.

The Soviet Union was not deterred by the fact that the United States spent half a million dollars and put a half a million troops into Vietnam. They went on their adventures during that period in the Middle East, Central America, Africa, and other parts of Southeast Asia.

The fundamental reality is that the United States's enemies are on the defensive. Osama bin Laden, its principle enemy, is dead. Al Qaeda has been decimated to the point that people don't even remember that there was this thing called al Qaeda. Al Qaeda was the principle enemy of the United States when Obama took office and was regarded as a fearsome terrorist organization, which is precisely the reason Obama has been brutal in his use of force against them. His administration was instrumental in the assassination of Osama bin Laden and also scores of other al Qaeda leaders from Pakistan to Yemen and beyond.

Who are America's other principal enemies? Iran is certainly one of them. When Obama came into office 75 percent of the Arabs who were polled — and not every Arab country was polled — looked favourably on Iran. Why? Because Iran stood up to the United States. If you remember the days of 2007 to 2008, anyone standing up to the Bush administration was seen as some kind of heroic figure. Today that number is down to 35 percent. Why? Because Obama assembled an international coalition to rein in Iran — to deal with the problem globally rather than as a purely American national interest issue. Iran is now at the negotiating table, by every expert's account making larger and greater concessions than it ever has made before.

Or take Russia. The Bush and Obama administrations were in similar situations with the country. Russia invaded Georgia at the end of the Bush administration and faced zero consequences. Even President Bush's supporters will admit it. What happened this past year? Again, Obama assembled a coalition of the Western countries, and for the first time got Europe to enact serious sanctions. The United States has enacted even more serious sanctions. Russia's growth rate is down to zero. Its stock market has tumbled. The ruble is down 25 percent. It is absolutely clear that Putin recognizes that these consequences of his intervention in Ukraine were more than he had bargained for.

But ask yourself was Obama tough on America's enemies when they did things that deserved some kind of U.S. response? I believe the answer is yes. Barack Obama has not initiated new and foolish wars. And if that's the measure of American strength then I think he would have to plead guilty.

RUDYARD GRIFFITHS: Let's talk about the debate within this debate. Critics are saying that Barack Obama is — to quote the title of your book — pulling America too quickly into the post-American world, but there is a Pax Americana that is still intact and that this president has abandoned it, to the peril of the American people and potentially to the peril of global stability.

FAREED ZAKARIA: Let's think about that statement. The most important piece of the Pax Americana is the ability of the United States to maintain global stability so that it can maintain the open global economic system and trading system. The single most important part of that premise would be to maintain stability in Asia. If the United States is going to have a relevant role in the twenty-first century — and I believe it will, because it is the single most important country — it will have to be a Pacific power to maintain stability in Asia.

So what has Barack Obama done in the region? He has, for the first time in thirty years, re-opened American bases in the Philippines as part of his pivot to Asia. This was previously unthinkable. He's put in place a small but symbolic and significant troop deployment in Australia. He has strengthened ties with Vietnam, the Philippines, and Japan. He has extended the U.S.-Japan security umbrella to clearly include those disputed islands that China has been coveting.

All these things have been part of a pivot to Asia, the most important pieces of which are an attempt to create a new trade agreement that would bind the free countries of Asia together even more closely. Some of this hasn't happened yet and some of it could be better.

But Obama has done a lot for the United States once you get away from all the day-to-day polemics. He has expanded America's security footprint in the most important theatre of the twenty-first century. That doesn't strike me as retreat — it strikes me as an aggressive expansion of American power and purpose in the area where it matters. He has not rushed headlong into the chaotic, unstable Middle East, which has sucked every American president dry for the last twenty-five years and would do so almost surely to this one. If that is how we define American strength, George Bush should be considered the president who presided over the greatest act in American diplomacy. And we know that was not true. The Iraq war was a disaster that weakened America. If Barack Obama chooses wisely to be careful about those kinds of commitments, he's doing something that will build American strength, not detract from it.

RUDYARD GRIFFITHS: When you think of this president entering his final two years, what to this date will stand out as his lasting contribution on the world stage?

FAREED ZAKARIA: I think there are probably two or three big achievements that will stand out, most notably his use of restraint.

Eisenhower refused to intervene in Suez or to help the Taiwanese in the Formosa Straits Crisis, which were extremely wise decisions that historians look back on with great admiration. They were wildly unpopular at the time and he was regarded as an appeaser. Similarly, I think Obama's willingness to be careful and considerate about the commitment of major U.S. forces or American military intervention abroad will be regarded as wise.

His second legacy is the determination with which he went after al Qaeda and associated terrorist organizations. He would likely target ISIL in a similar way were it to prove to be an actual threat to the United States and to Western countries, which I think the jury is still out on. It is a regional organization of disgruntled Sunnis in Iraq and Syria that has rhetorical ambitions beyond that.

And his third legacy will be the pivot to Asia — the attempt to recognize that the United States can only play the role that it needs to in the twenty-first century as the central power in the world if it is a Pacific power and is undergirding the stability of the Asia-Pacific. And no matter who his successor, whether it is a Democrat or Republican, I would argue he or she will continue Obama's policy toward Asia and terrorism.

RUDYARD GRIFFITHS: Great insights as always. Fareed Zakaria, thank you for coming to Toronto. We really look forward to the debate tonight.

FAREED ZAKARIA: Rudyard, my pleasure as always.

ANNE-MARIE SLAUGHTER IN CONVERSATION
WITH RUDYARD GRIFFITHS

RUDYARD GRIFFITHS: Anne-Marie Slaughter, you're an acclaimed scholar, someone who's served her government at the very highest levels in the State Department, and you're the head of New America, which we know as the New America Foundation; so just terrific to have you here in Toronto.

What I want to do is talk a little bit about the debate tonight and your views on the resolution at hand: "Be it resolved: President Obama has made the world a more dangerous place." We can't be more provocative than that. You think your opponents tonight need to prove a counterfactual.

ANNE-MARIE SLAUGHTER: Yes.

RUDYARD GRIFFITHS: And you don't think that's going to be easy. Give us a top-line sense of why you think they've got a steep hill to climb.

ANNE-MARIE SLAUGHTER: They have to argue that if someone else were president, Putin would not have invaded Crimea and then Ukraine. So you really have to make the case that he has emboldened Putin, Xi Jinping, or ISIL, and that's why the world is a more dangerous place.

And my proposition is that the world is a very dangerous place. There are a lot of things you can criticize Obama for. But take the Putin example: he invaded Ukraine for lots of reasons, not least of which is because he's weak at home and he needs to bolster his domestic standing, and is relying on nationalism to do that.

It's very hard to assume that if Barack Obama had done something different Putin wouldn't have acted as he did. So my point is they have to prove not just that Obama has made a difference, but that he's emboldened our enemies and caused them to do things they wouldn't have otherwise.

RUDYARD GRIFFITHS: Just to continue on Putin for a minute. Your opponents are going to connect Obama erasing his red line in the sand with Bashar al-Assad over a strike on chemical weapons views to Putin. They'll say, "Look, that inaction emboldened actors like Vladimir Putin because they'll believe America isn't in the red-line business anymore."

ANNE-MARIE SLAUGHTER: I have criticized Obama for not sticking to that particular red line. But if you analyze the chronology of Putin's invasion in Ukraine what you see is that Yanukovych fleeing is what made the biggest impact on him. And at that point the hard-liners around Putin said, "No matter what we do, this is how the U.S. will respond because they are in the business of overturning governments." So I think you have to show precisely how it is that our not doing something in Syria actually led Putin to invade.

RUDYARD GRIFFITHS: Barack Obama and your government are now doing air strikes in both northern Iraq and in Syria. Do you think that this president doesn't get enough credit for his hawkish side? He's painted as a dove, but look at the history of his actions, including a lot of unconventional warfare against al Qaeda, and his invasion of Libya — that doesn't seem so tame to me. If that's what a dove is today I'd hate to know what qualifies as a hawk.

ANNE-MARIE SLAUGHTER: Obama's acting where he is convinced he can make a difference. He's decimated al Qaeda, independent of killing Osama bin Laden; he supported the French action in Mali. In Libya he acted with NATO. And in the case of northern Iraq and Syria, he has the means to contain ISIL; whether he can eradicate them remains to be seen.

He's acting where he is certain that he can have an impact, and he's avoiding actions that in his mind would enflame our enemies. In other words, he knows that boots on the ground in the Middle East is the sure-fire way to make things worse — and there I agree with him. There are other instances where I think he could do more, but I don't think he's emboldening any enemies.

RUDYARD GRIFFITHS: How do you respond to the critics who say, "Air strikes for now — a policy of containment — but inevitably this is going to lead to boots on the ground because you can't get the results that you need from air strikes alone?" Do you think this is another example of Obama going halfway as opposed to all the way to do what really needs to be done?

ANNE-MARIE SLAUGHTER: Regardless of what political party you belong to, if our experience in Iraq and Afghanistan has taught us anything, it is that putting troops on the ground does not achieve a definitive answer — the longer you stay in a country the more complicated the situation gets. Yes, we could wipe out ISIL fighters temporarily, but they would come back the minute we leave.

We need to think about the objective. Can he keep ISIL so weak and so disorganized that they are unable to mount major attacks — either in Iraq, Europe, or the United States — and also weaken them in Syria? Yes. And he can do that from the air.

RUDYARD GRIFFITHS: Do you think that people who look at Obama's foreign policy record are not fully understanding the emergence of new types of threats — that we're still looking through the Cold War lens of the more traditional state actors? Have we forgotten that these new threats are very different?

ANNE-MARIE SLAUGHTER: I suspect you've been in my computer and read my closing statement, but I think that's absolutely right. The whole idea that one man could change the global system and embolden our enemies and make the world a more dangerous place is an idea that goes back to the last century, or even to the nineteenth century. Proponents of this line of thinking believe that Kaiser Wilhelm plunged the globe into World War I because Bismarck left, or that Hitler started World War II because of Neville Chamberlain's policy of appeasement. I'm not sure that was ever true, but it certainly isn't accurate now.

Russia and Iran's nuclear ambitions are in the landscape of real threats. But you also see climate change, pandemics, terrorist networks that are spontaneous in many places, and global criminal networks, not to mention the sort of even deeper problems of illiteracy and corruption that keep billions of people from essentially achieving peace and prosperity themselves.

Obama has been much savvier than recent presidents. He's understood the long-term causes of a lot of the current military threats we see and he's tried to address them. He's not getting very far on climate change, but not for lack of trying. He's elevated development. He's prioritized food security and health. He's on the front lines of Ebola, getting the rest of the world to act. These issues are just as grave threats as traditional state invasions.

RUDYARD GRIFFITHS: Beneath this debate, do you think there's an anxiety about the decline of America's power relative to other nations, such as China, and to a certain degree to Europe? When people are critical of this president, do you think they're feeling America's power slipping away from what they knew ten, twenty, or thirty years ago?

ANNE-MARIE SLAUGHTER: That's an interesting question. I see this happening more in Europe than I do in the United States. In other words, Americans by and large don't think we should be policing the world. They think we should be taking care of our own business. We've always had an isolationist streak and it's very strong now since we have a weak economy at home, or, more specifically, an economy that's not delivering for everyone. Americans are not sure of our purpose in the world right now, but we're pretty confident it shouldn't be fighting long wars in Iraq and Afghanistan. They want us to focus on fixing ourselves at home.

Foreign policy watchers like me are worried about decline, but I don't believe Americans as a whole are concerned.

RUDYARD GRIFFITHS: What happens in the final two years of this presidency? We saw mid-term election results that now have Republicans controlling both houses of Congress. Does this president act more forcefully abroad because he constitutionally can? Or do domestic priorities and concern for his own legacy now take over?

ANNE-MARIE SLAUGHTER: On the foreign policy side there are some things he can do now that he couldn't before. He is much more likely to get big trade deals, for example. Many Republicans in the Senate and the House will support trade deals with Europe and with parts of Asia, which is going to be very important for rebuilding some relationships.

I think you may also see a deal with Iran that Republicans will agree to. In terms of his legacy, it's hard to know. I do think he will do everything he can to defend Obamacare, which is his single biggest achievement.

RUDYARD GRIFFITHS: Final question: What do you think Obama's foreign policy legacy will be? Do you think there will be something that stands out?

ANNE-MARIE SLAUGHTER: He will be remembered for ending two wars. He got us out of the wars we were in and allowed us to concentrate on rebuilding at home. He stopped the bleeding, literally as well as figuratively. And he also will be remembered as the president who insisted on working through multilateral institutions to repair the damage that had been done by the really aggressive unilateralism of George W. Bush.

RUDYARD GRIFFITHS: Great. Anne-Marie Slaughter, thank you very much. I look forward to the debate tonight.

ANNE-MARIE SLAUGHTER: It's my pleasure.

ROBERT KAGAN IN CONVERSATION
WITH RUDYARD GRIFFITHS

RUDYARD GRIFFITHS: Ladies and gentlemen, welcome back to our pre-debate interviews. I'm here with Bob Kagan, senior fellow at the Brookings Institution, and one of America's most influential writers and commentators on foreign policy. Bob, you're arguing for this motion, "Be it resolved: President Obama has emboldened our enemies and made the world a more dangerous place." You were a student of history as well as policy. What is it about this particular president, as compared to other recent incumbents of this office, that you think has harmed or hurt America's standing on a world stage?

ROBERT KAGAN: I think he brings what you'd have to call a post–Cold War, maybe even a post–World War II, mindset to international relations for the United States. The United States basically picked up the role as global leader after World War II, and it really persisted for the next seventy years. I would argue he's the first American president who doesn't really buy that concept.

He reminds me much more of the presidents of the 1920s, like Harding or Coolidge, who had the same response to World War I that Barack Obama had to the Iraq War. They all pulled the United States back. It's not easy to do once you've taken control of a country like the United States. He has signalled both to the American people and to the world that he would like to pare back the American role, but unfortunately, in the international system where we live this creates all kinds of problems, including making allies uncertain and giving adversaries the feeling that they might be able to get away with aggressive behaviour.

RUDYARD GRIFFITHS: And how do you respond to those who say: "The world is a much more crowded place than it was after World War II. America's power has declined relative to other incumbents, like China, that are now in the field?" Isn't Obama simply acknowledging the times and the direction of global geopolitics?

ROBERT KAGAN: No. I don't accept the notion that America is really even in relative decline compared to the past. I don't envy the period of the Cold War, when the Soviet Union occupied half of Europe and had a massive nuclear arsenal aimed at the United States, and Mao and some of his successors ruled Communist China. I think we're actually better off, in theory, than we were back then.

China has its own difficulties. Russia is one of those countries that can cause a lot of trouble, but nobody actually thinks that the future belongs to Russia. The United States still has the capacity to shape the international system — not perfectly or with omnipotence, but it was never omnipotent. We were never able to do everything we wanted to do. It was always a struggle. And I think it's an unwillingness to undertake that struggle that has characterized recent years, but it is not unique to Obama. He's reflecting the public mood to a large extent. The American people have definitely gotten weary of playing this role, especially after the economic recession, but Obama has also encouraged this step back.

What's interesting is that the American people now have a very low opinion of President Obama's foreign policy, as low as for George Bush in 2006. My theory is the American people may have wanted this but they're not grateful to him for giving it to them.

RUDYARD GRIFFITHS: You talk about American weariness. A more active America in the world probably means an America more willing to intervene, to use military force, and to consider boots on the ground. Is that in the American mindset at all? Is it right to criticize Obama for being weary when this feeling is so pervasive and powerful?

ROBERT KAGAN: The American people have been known to change their minds. If you look at recent polls, he's gotten tremendous support for the use of force back in the Middle East, which is interesting. We've sent troops back into Iraq, and the American people are supportive.

I don't mean to be trite, but there is this thing called leadership. It reminds me of the dilemma that Franklin Roosevelt faced in the 1930s. America was a much more isolationist country and the public mood reflected that. And at first Roosevelt just went along with it. He didn't want to challenge the status quo. But as the risks and the dangers in the world increased, he did his best to educate the American people and bring them into the war, just in the nick of time. And of course, without Pearl Harbor who knows what would have happened?

It is a president's job to sometimes push against the prevailing winds. If the American people are too activist, sometimes you have to restrain them. But if they're too passive, sometimes you have to push them a little bit in the other direction. And as I say, Obama is more inclined just to go along with it.

Obama thought he was elected to focus on domestic issues, but unfortunately, as always happens to American presidents, foreign policies came to him whether he's happy about it or not.

RUDYARD GRIFFITHS: Let's talk about one of those foreign policy headaches: ISIL. Do you think the response has been adequate? He has intervened: it's not boots on the ground but it's a policy of containment backed up by significant air power.

ROBERT KAGAN: From the very beginning, even sitting military officials — including the chairman of the Joint Chiefs of Staff and others whom Obama has appointed — have been warning that air power alone will not be successful. They need trainers and advisers from the United States on the ground with the forces to call in air strikes, to help them make the right decisions. As of now, those air strikes have not really achieved much, even in terms of containment. The Yazidis we rescued from ISIL earlier this year are apparently now back up on the mountain and facing the same threats. There's been no progress in Syria at all.

I fear that President Obama has done enough to sort of make people think he's doing something but not necessarily enough to actually succeed. The price of that will be yet another military effort that didn't achieve much, and that would be very unfortunate, and would reinforce the American people's sense that we just can't do anything anymore, which has become pretty common in the American public's mind.

RUDYARD GRIFFITHS: Do you think threats are very different now than they have been in the past — sub-state actors that are asymmetrical and beyond borders? Has Obama tried to incorporate an understanding of these bigger twenty-first-century threats into his diplomacy and his approach to foreign policy? Is he getting it right?

ROBERT KAGAN: There's always something new happening in the world. Climate change is definitely a new challenge and I don't think we've addressed it very successfully. I don't see a lot of progress on the global agreement between the United States, China, Europe, and India on how exactly to proceed, but at least Obama's been addressing it.

As far as sub-state actors are concerned, the particular sub-state actor known as terrorism has been with us for quite a while and I would say it's reached a new level in a way. We've had groups operating within countries for at least a little while, but we now have a group that's threatening to become a country, if ISIL is able to carve out this caliphate that they're seeking. That is definitely new and Obama is not handling it well.

But there are also some very traditional geopolitical problems that have re-emerged after being quiescent for a while. Russia and Europe, running from the Baltic states through Ukraine to Georgia, is now contested territory. And we've already seen a very twentieth-century response from Vladimir Putin: he couldn't achieve his goals economically or politically so he just sent in the troops — we've seen that before.

In East Asia, we see a similar fault line in which China, a regionally rising power, wants to extend its influence in the same way other powers have traditionally done. It's similar to the Japan of the 1920s and 1930s, except that fault line now is between China and Japan on one side, and China and India on the other.

These are the kinds of geopolitical problems that I worry about. These are the kinds of things that really change the international order. It's when the great power conflicts begin to arise that things really start changing in ways that become out of our control. And that's what I'd like to try to get under control in the coming decade or so.

RUDYARD GRIFFITHS: Final question: What do you think this president's going to be remembered for in terms of his foreign policy?

ROBERT KAGAN: That's a very good question. Believe it or not, with two years left to go, who knows? I don't want to duck the question, but if you had asked how Ronald Reagan was going to look in 1987 at the height of the Iran-Contra Affair, everybody would have said, "Oh forget it. This guy's the worst." But after the scandal, he negotiated the Intermediate-Range Nuclear Forces Treaty (INF) with the Soviet Union. And suddenly in 1989 the Soviet Union collapsed and everything looked different. I'm a little hesitant to answer definitively because two years is a long time.

I would say that he may be remembered for shifting the pendulum too far. After George Bush's two terms there needed to be a corrective. But did he take the corrective too far in the other direction, and instead of coming up with a kind of intelligent but persistent American engagement, a willingness to use force when necessary but in an intelligent way, did we go all the way over to — in his words — "nation-building at home not active involvement abroad?" That's one possibility.

RUDYARD GRIFFITHS: Robert Kagan, I look forward to the debate tonight. Thank you for coming to Toronto.

BRET STEPHENS IN CONVERSATION
WITH RUDYARD GRIFFITHS

RUDYARD GRIFFITHS: I'm here with Bret Stephens, distinguished columnist with the *Wall Street Journal*, author of a big new book called *America in Retreat: The New Isolationism and the Coming Global Disorder*. He is also the former editor-in-chief of the *Jerusalem Post*. I want to talk to you about tonight's debate. Your critics are going to say, "The world's a messy place and this president inherited a legacy from George W. Bush. You're being too tough on him and not being a realist."

BRET STEPHENS: Every president inherits a messy legacy. Reagan inherited a mess from Carter, Nixon from Johnson. Franklin Roosevelt certainly inherited a tough hand from Hoover. But the mark of a great president isn't the legacy he's dealt; it's his ability to shape and define an agenda and to meet the goals that he sets for himself at the beginning of his term.

Think about what those goals were for President Obama. He wanted to defeat al Qaeda. He was going to get us out of the dumb war in Iraq. And we were going to win the war that had to be won in Afghanistan. He wanted to reset relations with Russia and to mend frayed ties with our European, North American, and Latin American partners. He also wanted to combat climate change and stop Iran's nuclear program. The list goes on and on. He promised a great deal.

Think about where we are today. Not one of those goals is even close to being achieved. On the contrary, we've moved in the opposite direction. We've reset relations with Russia to 1956. Al Qaeda is on an awfully long path to defeat — if at all. A study in Iran just came out showing that the number of jihadists in the world doubled between 2010 and 2013.

So, yes, every president inherits a situation and every president has to deal with events. And I'm not making an argument that Obama should have had perfect command of events and that everything would go his way, but there's a consistency of failure here that is almost unprecedented among recent U.S. presidents.

RUDYARD GRIFFITHS: And what's to blame for that? Is this something particular to his strategy — this idea of the limited use of force, a hesitancy toward intervention? Do you think it's the lack of a more muscular foreign policy that's to blame?

BRET STEPHENS: Part of the problem, and I'm quoting my opponent Anne-Marie Slaughter here, is that Obama is a president who meets bullets with words. After Russia invaded Ukraine and seized Crimea, Obama went to Europe and delivered a superb speech reminding us of the lessons of 1914 and how you can't allow aggression to remain unchecked. And yet, aggression went effectively unchecked. It was the same story, of course, in Syria. A red line was set and then there were no consequences when that line was crossed. The only difference is that Assad started killing people with chlorine gas as opposed to sarin gas.

What we have is a world in which America's foes — the foes of the West — don't think that American threats are credible. And we have friends who don't believe American assurances are credible. And that's a dangerous world to live in because it means that your foes are going to take advantage of you sooner rather than later. Knowing that Obama has just two years to go in office, our friends might start freelancing their foreign policy.

We've talked about the possibility of an Israeli strike on Iran, but what if Saudi Arabia concludes that the United States isn't serious about stopping the Iranians and tests or fields a nuclear arsenal of its own? They can do it. Do we really want a Middle East where the Saudis also have a bomb? This is how Obama makes the world dangerous.

RUDYARD GRIFFITHS: But in these instances you've just talked about, do you think that there would have been an appetite in Congress or among the American people for military intervention in eastern Ukraine, Crimea, or Syria? In other words, does this president even have the mandate from his own institutions and the public to act in the way that you think he should have?

BRET STEPHENS: I think there's no doubt that to some extent the president's Republican opponents in Congress have participated in some of these debacles, not least the breached or the broken red line in Syria. Nonetheless, Americans typically expect their presidents to lead. In domestic politics, the president has to act according to the polls.

If you had asked Americans six months ago, "Do you want to intervene or help the Ukrainians stave off Russian aggression?" or "What do you want to do about Syria?" you probably would have gotten a lot of public pushback suggesting that they were weary of war. And yet, paradoxically, or maybe not so paradoxically, you now find that the president's ratings on foreign policy are at a new low. In fact, it was probably among his biggest liabilities in the recent November elections. Why? Because Americans sense that the country is weaker than ever, that it's being disrespected, and that our enemies are gathering strength and taking advantage of our perceived weaknesses.

RUDYARD GRIFFITHS: A truly depressing, but I think pressing piece of your analysis of this whole situation is that America may now actually have to use force. It may have to act in a forthright and direct way precisely to restore its credibility, that it's been backed into this problem now.

BRET STEPHENS: That's a terrific point. Churchill famously said, "Better jaw-jaw than war-war," but you can only jaw-jaw if your adversaries think that there is some substance behind the words. We've arrived at this point of diminished credibility where adversaries are going to be tempted to test what our real red lines are. And how do you restore these limits? You can't do it with another speech or another round of weak sanctions.

Let's imagine that Vladimir Putin wants to really break the back of NATO and seizes a portion of Estonia, which has a large Russian ethnic minority just like Ukraine does, or some of the other Baltic states, which are currently almost indefensible. What would we really be prepared to do? We've reached that point because the Budapest Memorandum on Security Assurances promised Ukraine its territorial integrity in 1994 in exchange for them giving up their hold over a nuclear arsenal. Those assurances are now in doubt.

So an American president needs to make sure that he draws his red lines sparingly but that they're credible when he does. And now we've crossed a Rubicon and the president is going to have a hard time restoring that sense that we're a country that means business, whether on Iran, the South China Sea, or the Baltics.

RUDYARD GRIFFITHS: What do you think is going to happen in the final two years of this presidency? The Democrats just lost the Senate in the mid-terms. He's going to face off against a more powerful and emboldened Republican Party. Does that mean that foreign policy takes on more importance for him because he constitutionally has more latitude to act? Or is this a president that hunkers down and gets into legacy mode?

BRET STEPHENS: I hope it's the latter and that he decides two years of constructive bipartisanship will do the history of his presidency some good. There are things that he could do that would be fantastic, like really push the TPP, which has been dormant on the agenda. Or, if there is a failure to reach an agreement with Iranians in November, or if the deal is deemed unacceptable, that he adopt what Congress was trying to do earlier this year, which was re-impose real sanctions with teeth on Iranians so they are forced to make a fundamental choice. They can have a bomb or a regime, but not both. And that would generate a great deal of bipartisan support.

My fear is that he's going to want to hold on tight and do what he can to make sure a Democrat is elected two years from now, and secure his domestic legacy. There's a famous saying: "Prediction is very difficult, especially about the future," so I'll leave it there.

RUDYARD GRIFFITHS: Final question: I'm going to ask you to predict again. What do you think he'll be remembered for internationally? What singular act or event do you think will define his presidency on the world stage in the history books?

BRET STEPHENS: Well if, God forbid, the presidency were to end today, I think he would be remembered as the president who ushered us not into a post-American world, as Fareed Zakaria put it, but into a post–Pax Americana world. Since the end of the Second World War we've lived in a world where the United States, sometimes wisely and smartly, sometimes less so, was the backstop country — the guarantor of a secure liberal international order that on the margins favoured freedom, defended small countries, and deterred aggressive states. If he were to leave office now I think he would be seen as the president who walked us out of that period, and I don't think we're in a good place. The next president is going to have to undo a lot of the damage he did. Hillary Clinton said, "'Don't do stupid stuff' is not an organizing principle for a great nation." The next president is going to have to come up with a sensible organizing principle for the country. For better or worse, the United States will remain a superpower for the rest of our lives, so he will be leaving a heavy burden on his successor.

RUDYARD GRIFFITHS: Great, Bret, perfect point to end our conversation. Thanks for coming to Toronto. I look forward to the debate tonight.

BRET STEPHENS: Thank you for having me.

Post-Debate Commentary

POST-DEBATE COMMENTARY
BY JOHN STACKHOUSE

Barack Obama is a hard man to defend these days — unless you're in Toronto.

At the latest Munk Debate, arguing the failure of Obama's foreign policy, you wouldn't know that the president was deeply unpopular at home and abroad, or that his party had just been routed in mid-term elections. The wheels of his foreign policy — democratic reform in the Middle East, carbon caps globally, free trade in the Pacific, a reset with Russia — can be found in the ditch, deflated, punctured, in some cases shredded. "Yes, we can" has given way to "No, you don't."

Except in Canada.

Against worse odds than a Democrat would face in Missouri, Fareed Zakaria and Anne-Marie Slaughter convinced more than two-thirds of the audience that Obama's foreign policy had not emboldened America's enemies and had not made the world a riskier place.

They even persuaded one in ten members of the audience to change their minds.

Consider the evidence that they had to overcome:

1. Obama went to Cairo in 2009 and proclaimed a new dawn for the Arab world, an age in which free speech and human rights would triumph. Today, Syria and Iraq are in free fall, Libya is in chaos, Yemen is on the verge of sectarian civil war, Egypt is in the military's grip, and Jordan and Lebanon hang perilously in the balance.
2. Iran has more nuclear weapons materials than ever.
3. Russia is an aggressor and adversary of America again.
4. Japan, America's most significant ally in the Pacific, is starting to go its own way.
5. The Intergovernmental Panel on Climate Change (IPCC) sounded its most serious alarm yet this week, because nothing significant had been done to curb carbon emissions.

As *Foreign Policy* magazine noted this week, "Obama will reap the results of his political and policy narcissism in a way that will not only be difficult for him personally but will be bad for America and its role in the world." You would think the "pro" side — conservative stalwarts Robert Kagan of the Brookings Institution and Bret Stephens from the *Wall Street Journal* — would have a walk in the park. But they didn't properly account for the Canadian bias. At the beginning of the evening,

57 percent of voters said they opposed the resolution that the president had made the world more dangerous.

After ninety minutes of evidence and argument, 68 percent stood with the opposition.

What gave?

In many ways, rhetoric won the evening, as is so often the case with Obama. Zakaria waxed wit and optimism for an American century that gives more than it takes. Yes, there are serious pockets of instability — always have been and always will be.

Slaughter was less sure on her feet, having written many condemnations of Obama's foreign policy, but she managed to cling faithfully to the "dealt a bad hand" argument. She compared blaming Obama for the insecure state of the world to blaming a Caribbean island for being hit by a hurricane, a clever twist on the school of root causes. Hurricane Sykes-Picot, perhaps. For good measure, she also rolled out a "he's trying his best" argument, citing climate change and free trade as policy initiatives that deserve an A for effort.

Kagan countered with a litany of the president's failures: a premature withdrawal from Iraq; the ridiculed red line in Syria; mayhem in Ukraine. Who could dispute that America's enemies — Assad, Khamenei, Putin — are bolder today than five years ago? The former Red Army is on the move, the mullahs of Tehran have nuclear materials, and the Assad regime has chemical weapons, so surely the world is less safe.

Is that Obama's fault? The counterfactual arguments got less debate than they should have. What if Obama

had not been in power? What if a unilateralist or isolationist ran the White House? Would American forces in
Iraq or Syria make the world safer, or even discourage
the enemy? Conversely, would a stay-at-home president
make Ukraine less tempting to Putin?

The audience didn't buy it. They seemed to see mud-
dling through as a reasonable option, even at the cost of
some chaos. Foreign policy analysts have called the Obama
preference for ad hoc coalitions that put the goal of mini-
mizing damage ahead of all else "messy-lateralism."
Inspiring to all, no; securing to some, yes.

Slaughter stressed her side's point with an incisive
critique of the Great Man School, the one espoused by
those who want linear strategies and singular outcomes.
The twenty-first century, she said, is too crowded and
complex for single actions and actors to prevail. It is
an age of networks and non-state actors, from jihadists and private armies to multinationals and oligarchs.
Presidents, at best, can co-ordinate and referee.

Zakaria may have won the evening with a more
sweeping view — his speciality. He agreed Syria is a
mess and that Obama has not done anything to make
it better, but Syria is not the world and the majority of
people today are in a more secure spot politically, socially,
and economically than they were in 2008. China, India,
Indonesia, Mexico, South America, Nigeria, East Africa,
and Southern Africa are all largely out of the news
because they're doing okay.

So even if the evidence is compelling that America's
enemies have been emboldened, and global security

jeopardized, a pro-Obama room needed more to turn. It needed to be persuaded that his absence would have made things worse.

In the end, there was no need for a count. The crowd's mood was obvious during Stephens's arguments, in which he paid tribute to the Canadian bombing runs underway in Iraq, a note of thanks from an American that might have drawn some patriotic cheers elsewhere. Instead, the applause line garnered only a polite response.

Like Obama, the Munk audience seemed content with caution, even on the way to the exit.

John Stackhouse is a senior fellow at the Munk School of Global Affairs and the C. D. Howe Institute, and former editor-in-chief of the Globe and Mail.

POST-DEBATE COMMENTARY BY JANICE STEIN

The latest Munk Debate was supposed to be about whether President Obama has emboldened our enemies and made the world a more dangerous place. The four debaters, however, quickly zeroed in on an age-old question: they argued all evening about whether leaders are the victims of history or whether they make and shape it.

Even those who spoke in favour of the resolution — Bret Stephens and Robert Kagan — conceded that Barack Obama had inherited a tough hand. When he became president, the world had just gone through a terrible economic crisis, Iran was rushing ahead with its nuclear program, and America was at war in Iraq and Afghanistan. Nevertheless, the president, they argued, promised to avoid a world recession, to reset relations with Russia, to remove Iran's capacity to make a nuclear weapon, and to end America's wars and bring home the troops. Obama, they insisted, has met none of these objectives and, on the contrary, emboldened his enemies.

They conceded the argument made by Anne-Marie Slaughter and Fareed Zakaria that the president has led a vigorous economic recovery in the United States, but everywhere else, they asserted, the president has failed to meet the objectives he set himself.

Most important, America is at war again, against the much larger and better-armed Islamic State, and it is at war in both Syria and Iraq because of the feckless decision the president made to stand back and refuse to help those fighting Bashir al-Assad in the early days. Even Anne-Marie Slaughter, arguing against the resolution, conceded that the president had made a mistake when he stood aside. Saudi Arabia, Qatar, and Iran filled the vacuum Obama created by arming militants who today constitute the shock troops of the Islamic State that has swept through northern Iraq and eastern Syria. Not so fast, countered Fareed Zakaria: the Syrian story is one similar to Saddam Hussein's Iraq, where a minority regime that ruled the majority through fear and brutality collapsed. On this issue, the two debaters who insisted that the president has not made the world worse seemed to be arguing with each other rather than with their opponents. The house of Obama was divided among itself.

Two other issues dominated the debate. What, the debaters argued, motivated President Vladimir Putin to shake Europe to its core by using force against Ukraine to unilaterally change Russia's borders? Those who see leaders as buffeted by the forces of history — Slaughter and Zakaria — argued that Putin was motivated largely by events in his neighbourhood and by domestic politics. When Obama had to move he did, and he put in place a robust set of sanctions. Not so, replied Kagan and Stephens. Obama emboldened Putin by his failure to keep his word after he drew a red line on the use of chemical weapons in Syria. Putin then called Obama's bluff and won. The newly assertive Russia was not Obama's fault, they conceded, but the president made it worse. Presidents have to shape history when history calls. Point taken.

The other big issue was a resurgent China in a globally important but twitchy Asia. Zakaria made a compelling argument that, early on, Obama got the importance of the United States as a Pacific power, announced a "pivot" to Asia, and established bases in Australia and the Philippines to reassure Asian allies jittery about China's vigorous assertion of claims in the South China Sea. Score one for good intentions. Kagan and Stephens responded vigorously by asking: "Where's the beef?" There has been no redeployment of forces to Asia, as the United States is caught up, yet again, in the ferocious sectarian fighting in the Middle East. Japan's leaders are deeply worried about China and deeply uncertain about the worth of a U.S. guarantee. Not only Japan, but Korea, Taiwan, and the Philippines all doubt American resolve and are increasingly willing to go their own way. Not only has Obama emboldened his enemies, the "pro" side concluded, but he has also alienated his friends. It is not what the president says that matters, but what he does. Score zero for execution.

Canada was but a footnote in the debate. Bret Stephens praised Canada for its contribution to the battle from the skies against the Islamic State, and the reaction of the crowd was polite but unenthusiastic. Fareed Zakaria spoke about a multilateral, peacekeeping, "good" Canada and the crowd roared. That Canada did exist once, in a different world way back in the twentieth century, but certainly not in the second decade of the twenty-first. Score zero for the audience.

The audience clearly favoured the argument that history shapes the leader, but that misses an important part of the story. Leaders shape events, and great leaders change the flow and the course of history. That we had such a vigorous and spirited debate tells us that, at least for now, Barack Obama does not rank as one of the great presidents.

Janice Stein is Director, Munk School of Global Affairs.

ACKNOWLEDGEMENTS

The Munk Debates are the product of the public-spiritedness of a remarkable group of civic-minded organizations and individuals. First and foremost, these debates would not be possible without the vision and leadership of the Aurea Foundation. Founded in 2006 by Peter and Melanie Munk, the Aurea Foundation supports Canadian individuals and institutions involved in the study and development of public policy. The debates are the foundation's signature initiative, a model for the kind of substantive public policy conversation Canadians can foster globally. Since the creation of the debates in 2008, the foundation has underwritten the entire cost of each semi-annual event. The debates have also benefited from the input and advice of members of the board of the foundation, including Mark Cameron, Andrew Coyne, Devon Cross, Allan Gotlieb, George Jonas, Margaret MacMillan, Anthony Munk, Robert Prichard, and Janice Stein.

For her contribution to the preliminary edit of the book, the debate organizers would like to thank Jane McWhinney.

Since their inception the Munk Debates have sought to take the discussions that happen at each event to national and international audiences. Here the debates have benefited immeasurably from a partnership with Canada's national newspaper, the *Globe and Mail*, and the counsel of its editor-in-chief, David Walmsley.

With the publication of this superb book, House of Anansi Press is helping the debates reach new audiences in Canada and around the world. The debates' organizers would like to thank Anansi chair Scott Griffin and president and publisher Sarah MacLachlan for their enthusiasm for this book project and insights into how to translate the spoken debate into a powerful written intellectual exchange.

ABOUT THE DEBATERS

BRET STEPHENS is a foreign affairs columnist and deputy editorial page editor responsible for the international opinion pages at the *Wall Street Journal.* He has won the Pulitzer Prize for distinguished commentary for his writing on U.S. foreign policy and been named a Young Global Leader by the World Economic Forum. He was previously editor-in-chief of the *Jerusalem Post* and is a regular panelist on the *Journal Editorial Report,* a weekly political talk show on Fox News.

ROBERT KAGAN is a senior fellow of foreign policy at the Brookings Institution's Center on the United States and Europe and a transatlantic fellow at the German Marshall Fund. *Foreign Policy* and *Prospect* listed him as one of the world's "Top 100 Intellectuals." Kagan served in the U.S. State Department as a deputy for policy in the Bureau of Inter-American Affairs, and was a principal speechwriter to the U.S. secretary of state. He is also the author of several bestselling books on foreign policy, including *Dangerous Nation*, which won the Lepgold Book Prize and was a finalist for the Lionel Gelber Prize.

FAREED ZAKARIA is host of CNN's flagship international affairs program, *Fareed Zakaria GPS*, which won the 2012 Peabody Award. He is also the editor-at-large of *Time*, contributing editor at the *Atlantic*, a *Washington Post* columnist, and a former editor of *Newsweek International*. He is the author of the international bestsellers *The Future of Freedom* and *The Post-American World: Release 2.0*. He was described by *Esquire* as "the most influential foreign policy adviser of his generation" and was included on *Foreign Policy*'s list of "Top 100 Global Thinkers."

ANNE-MARIE SLAUGHTER is the CEO of the New America Foundation, one of America's largest international affairs think tanks. She is the past dean of the Woodrow Wilson School of Public and International Affairs at Princeton and served as director of policy planning for the U.S. State Department from 2009–11. She has been named one of *Foreign Policy*'s "Top 100 Global Thinkers" and is the author and editor of six books, including *A New World Order* and *The Idea That Is America*.

ABOUT THE EDITOR

RUDYARD GRIFFITHS is chair of the Munk Debates and president of the Aurea Foundation. In 2006 he was named one of Canada's "Top 40 under 40" by the *Globe and Mail*. He is the editor of thirteen books on history, politics, and international affairs, including *Who We Are: A Citizen's Manifesto*, which was a *Globe and Mail* Best Book of 2009 and a finalist for the Shaughnessy Cohen Prize for Political Writing. He lives in Toronto with his wife and two children.

ABOUT THE AUTHOR

EDWARD GREENSPAN was the winner of the World Debating and Public Speaking Championship. In 2006, he was named one of Canada's "Ten to Watch" by the *Globe and Mail*. He is the editorial director of books on history, politics, and international affairs, including *War, Nobserved* and *Crazy About Lili*, which won the *Stephen Leacock Book Prize* and was a finalist for the *National Magazine Prize for Political Writing*. He lives in Toronto with his wife and two children.

ABOUT THE MUNK DEBATES

The Munk Debates are Canada's premier public policy event. Held semi-annually, the debates provide leading thinkers with a global forum to discuss the major public policy issues facing the world and Canada. Each event takes place in Toronto in front of a live audience, and the proceedings are covered by domestic and international media. Participants in recent Munk Debates include Robert Bell, Tony Blair, John Bolton, Ian Bremmer, Daniel Cohn-Bendit, Paul Collier, Howard Dean, Hernando de Soto, Alan Dershowitz, Maureen Dowd, Gareth Evans, Mia Farrow, Niall Ferguson, William Frist, Newt Gingrich, David Gratzer, Glenn Greenwald, Michael Hayden, Rick Hillier, Christopher Hitchens, Richard Holbrooke, Josef Joffe, Henry Kissinger, Charles Krauthammer, Paul Krugman, Arthur Laffer, Lord Nigel Lawson, Stephen Lewis, David Li, Bjørn Lomborg, Lord Peter Mandelson, Elizabeth May, George Monbiot, Caitlin Moran,

Dambisa Moyo, Vali Nasr, Alexis Ohanian, Camille Paglia, George Papandreou, Samantha Power, David Rosenberg, Hanna Rosin, Lawrence Summers, Amos Yadlin, and Fareed Zakaria.

The Munk Debates are a project of the Aurea Foundation, a charitable organization established in 2006 by philanthropists Peter and Melanie Munk to promote public policy research and discussion. For more information, visit www.munkdebates.com.

ABOUT THE INTERVIEWS

Rudyard Griffith's interviews with Fareed Zakaria, Anne-Marie Slaughter, Robert Kagan, and Bret Stephens were recorded on November 5, 2014. The Aurea Foundation is gratefully acknowledged for permission to reprint excerpts from the following:

ABOUT THE POST-DEBATE COMMENTARY

John Stackhouse's and Janice Stein's post-debate commentaries were written on November 6, 2014. The Aurea Foundation wishes to thank Rudyard Griffiths for his assistance in commissioning these essays.

(p. 85) "Post-Debate Commentary," by John Stackhouse. Copyright © 2015 Aurea Foundation.

(p. 91) "Post-Debate Commentary," by Janice Stein. Copyright © 2015 Aurea Foundation.

Does State Spying Make Us Safer?
Hayden and Dershowitz vs. Greenwald and Ohanian

In a risk-filled world, democracies are increasingly turning to large-scale state surveillance, at home and abroad, to fight complex and unconventional threats. Former head of the CIA and NSA Michael Hayden and civil liberties lawyer Alan Dershowitz square off against journalist Glenn Greenwald and reddit co-founder Alexis Ohanian to debate if the government should be able to monitor our activities in order to keep us safe.

"Surveillance equals power. The more you know about someone, the more you can control and manipulate them in all sorts of ways."

— Glenn Greenwald

www.houseofanansi.com/munkdebates

Are Men Obsolete?
Rosin and Dowd vs. Moran and Paglia

For the first time in history, will it be better to be a woman than a man in the upcoming century? Renowned author and editor Hanna Rosin and Pulitzer Prize–winning columnist Maureen Dowd challenge *New York Times*–bestselling author Caitlin Moran and trailblazing social critic Camille Paglia to debate the relative decline of the power and status of men in the workplace, the family, and society at large.

"Feminism was always wrong to pretend women could 'have it all.' It is not male society but Mother Nature who lays the heaviest burden on women."

— Camille Paglia

Should We Tax the Rich More?
Krugman and Papandreou vs. Gingrich and Laffer

Is imposing higher taxes on the wealthy the best way for countries to reinvest in their social safety nets, education, and infrastructure while protecting the middle class? Or does raising taxes on society's wealth creators lead to capital flight, falling government revenues, and less money for the poor? Nobel Prize–winning economist Paul Krugman and former prime minister of Greece George Papandreou square off against former Speaker of the U.S. House of Representatives Newt Gingrich and famed economist Arthur Laffer to debate this key issue.

"The effort to finance big government through higher taxes is a direct assault on civil society."

— Newt Gingrich

www.houseofanansi.com/munkdebates

Can the World Tolerate an Iran with Nuclear Weapons?
Krauthammer and Yadlin vs. Zakaria and Nasr

Is the case for a pre-emptive strike on Iran ironclad? Or can a nuclear Iran be a stabilizing force in the Middle East? Former Israel Defense Forces head of military intelligence Amos Yadlin, Pulitzer Prize–winning political commentator Charles Krauthammer, CNN host Fareed Zakaria, and Iranian-born academic Vali Nasr debate the consequences of a nuclear-armed Iran.

"Deterring Iran is fundamentally different from deterring the Soviet Union. You could rely on the latter but not the former."
— Charles Krauthammer

North America's Lost Decade?
Krugman and Rosenberg vs. Summers and Bremmer

The future of the North American economy is more uncertain than ever. In this edition of the Munk Debates, Nobel Prize–winning economist Paul Krugman and chief economist and strategist at Gluskin Sheff + Associates David Rosenberg square off against former U.S. Treasury secretary Lawrence Summers and bestselling author Ian Bremmer to tackle the resolution: Be it resolved North America faces a Japan-style era of high unemployment and slow growth.

"It's now impossible to deny the obvious, which is that we are not now, and have never been, on the road to recovery."
— Paul Krugman

www.houseofanansi.com/munkdebates

Does the 21st Century Belong to China?
Kissinger and Zakaria vs. Ferguson and Li

Is China's rise unstoppable? Former U.S. secretary of state Henry Kissinger and CNN's Fareed Zakaria pair off against leading historian Niall Ferguson and world-renowned Chinese economist David Daokui Li to debate China's emergence as a global force, the key geopolitical issue of our time.

This edition of the Munk Debate on China is the first formal public debate Dr. Kissinger has participated in on China's future.

"I have enormous difficulty imagining a world dominated by China . . . I believe the concept that any one country will dominate the world is, in itself, a misunderstanding of the world in which we live now."

— Henry Kissinger

Hitchens vs. Blair
Christopher Hitchens vs. Tony Blair

Intellectual juggernaut and staunch atheist Christopher Hitchens goes head-to-head with former British prime minister Tony Blair, one of the Western world's most openly devout political leaders, on the age-old question: Is religion a force for good in the world? Few world leaders have had a greater hand in shaping current events than Blair; few writers have been more outspoken and polarizing than Hitchens.

Sharp, provocative, and thoroughly engrossing, *Hitchens vs. Blair* is a rigorous and electrifying intellectual sparring match on the contentious questions that continue to dog the topic of religion in our globalized world.

"If religious instruction were not allowed until the child had attained the age of reason, we would be living in a very different world."

— Christopher Hitchens

The Munk Debates: Volume One
Edited by Rudyard Griffiths; Introduction by Peter Munk

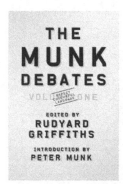

Launched in 2008 by philanthropists Peter and Melanie Munk, the Munk Debates is Canada's premier international debate series, a highly anticipated cultural event that brings together the world's brightest minds.

This volume includes the first five debates in the series, and features twenty leading thinkers and doers arguing for or against provocative resolutions that address pressing public policy concerns, such as the future of global security, the implications of humanitarian intervention, the effectiveness of foreign aid, the threat of climate change, and the state of health care in Canada and the United States.

"By trying to highlight the most important issues at crucial moments in the global conversation, these debates not only profile the ideas and solutions of some of our brightest thinkers and doers, but crystallize public passion and knowledge, helping to tackle some global challenges confronting humankind."

— Peter Munk

www.houseofanansi.com/munkdebates